Anahi
Ceja

California
Everyday Mathematics®

CALIFORNIA

The University of Chicago School Mathematics Project

My Reference Book

California Data Bank

California Content Standards

Let's visit some fun places in California. What is **in front of** you? What is **near?** What is **far?** Where in California are you?

▲ The coast of Santa Catalina Island

Come fly **above** the crowd! Look **down** at the people **below.** Where in California are you?

▲ A fair in the state capital, Sacramento

Take a ride in a cable car. Look out the window. What do you see as you ride **up** the hill? Where in California are you?

Chinatown in San Francisco ▲

Let's visit some polar bears. One polar bear is **above** the water on a rock. The slide **next to** the polar bear leads to the water **below.**

▲ The zoo in San Diego

Another polar bear is **inside** the cave. Where in California are you?

Stand at the top of this slide. What is **behind** you? What is **in front of** you? Pick a color and glide **down.** What color is to the **right of** you? What color is to the **left of** you? Where in California are you?

A county fair in Costa Mesa ➤

What places have *you* visited in California?

Shapes are everywhere. All over California, you can see shapes in buildings and other structures people have made. Some shapes can be put together to make other shapes.

What shapes do you see on this dome?

EI·AC·MELLIS

▲ The dome of the California Building in San Diego

In this bridge, triangles are put together to make other shapes. Where do small triangles make larger triangles? Squares? Rectangles?

▲ The Golden Gate Bridge in San Francisco

CALIFORNIA

Look for rectangles
in this building.
How many different
sizes of rectangles
do you see?

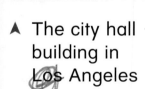

▲ The city hall
building in
Los Angeles

A pagoda is a tower with a
roof at every level. Many
trapezoids form this
pagoda. What other shapes
can you find in the pagoda?

▲ A pagoda in
San Francisco's
Chinatown

MRP

These are Victorian houses. How many different shapes do you see in them?

▲ Victorian houses in San Francisco

▲ A house on Eureka's
Victorian Row

What shapes can you find in the buildings where *you* live?

California Animals

The animals listed in the table below are native to California.

Average Animal Sizes

Animals of many different sizes are found in California. Compare the weights of the animals in the table. Which animal weighs the most? Which animals weigh the least?

Animal	Average Length	Average Weight
Big brown bat	3 in.	less than 1 lb
California newt	8 in.	less than 1 lb
Coyote	3 ft	3 lb
Desert tortoise	1 ft	12 lb
Gray whale	45 ft	70,000 lb
Grizzly bear	6 ft	750 lb
Harbor seal	6 ft	245 lb

Compare the lengths of the animals in the table. Which animal is the longest? Which animal is the shortest?

California Animal Facts

Many animals live in California. Here are some interesting facts about these native California animals.

A **big brown bat** cannot see its prey. It uses sound to find food. Big brown bats catch food while flying as fast as 40 miles per hour.

Big Brown Bat

A **California newt** gives off poison from its skin when it is scared. This protects it from enemies. A newt can live up to 55 years.

California Newt

A **coyote** baby is called a pup. A coyote pup is blind for the first 10 days of its life.

Coyote

Desert Tortoise

A **desert tortoise** can live without water for 1 year.

Gray Whale

A **gray whale** baby is called a calf. Gray whale calves can be 15 feet long and weigh 1,500 pounds when they are born.

Grizzly Bear

A **grizzly bear** can smell food 1 mile away.

Harbor Seal

A **harbor seal** does not chew its food. It swallows between 10 and 18 pounds of food each day in large chunks.

California Flowers

These flowers grow in many parts of California. Read on to find out more about these California flowers.

Bird-of-Paradise

The **bird-of-pardise** flower is a member of the banana family. A bird-of-paradise plant can grow up to 5 feet tall.

All the parts of a **calla lily** are harmful if eaten. Calla lilies grow on land that is as high as 984 feet above sea level.

Calla Lily

Golden Poppy

A **golden poppy** closes at night and opens again each morning. It was named the state flower of California in 1903.

Hedgehog Cactus

A **hedgehog cactus** grows fruit that tastes like strawberries. The pink flowers on the cactus can grow up to 4 inches long.

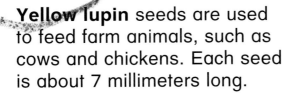

Yellow lupin seeds are used to feed farm animals, such as cows and chickens. Each seed is about 7 millimeters long.

Yellow Lupin

California Shells

More than 250 kinds of animals that have shells live in the water along the California coast.

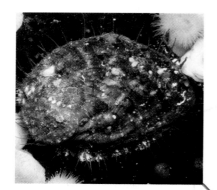

Abalone have tongues that are covered with thousands of teeth. They use their tongues to scrape algae off rocks.

Abalone

There are over 600 different kinds of cone snails. A **California cone snail** can sting.

California Cone Snail

California Mussel

The shell of a **California mussel** grows up to 5 inches long. It takes 3 years for this shell to reach its full size.

A **Pacific pink scallop** has a shell that is about 3 inches long. The shell is often covered with sponges, which help hide and protect the scallop.

Pacific Pink Scallop

Pacific Razor Clam

Pacific razor clams can bury themselves in the sand in less than 7 seconds.

San Diego Zoo

The San Diego Zoo and the Wild Animal Park are great places to visit. The zoo is home to more than 870 different kinds of animals.

Exhibits

Monkey Trails and Forest Tales

More than 30 different kinds of animals from Africa and Asia live in this exhibit.

Mandrills are large African monkeys with purple and blue markings, red lips, and golden beards. Male mandrills weigh about 55 pounds, while females weigh only about 25 pounds.

Rain Forest Aviary

The aviary looks like a real Southeast Asian rain forest. Almost 200 birds move freely around the exhibit.

See jacanas run across lily pads. These birds weigh from $1\frac{1}{2}$ ounces to 9 ounces. The females weigh 2 times more than the males.

Ituri Forest

This area looks like an African rain forest. It has a hippo pool that holds more than 150,000 gallons of water. Monkeys, birds, and fruit bats live in the large fig trees.

The hippo is the second heaviest mammal on earth. Hippos weigh about 100 pounds when they are born. An adult male can weigh more than 7,000 pounds.

Reptile Mesa

Walk around the Reptile Mesa and safely see cobras, pythons, and rattlesnakes.

Galapagos tortoises measure up to 6 feet from head to tail. The tortoises may live to be 150 years old.

Scientists know of more than 4,000 kinds of frogs and toads. At the mesa, see small, brightly colored poison-dart frogs.

Getting Around the Zoo

In the summer, the San Diego Zoo is open from 9:00 A.M. to 8:00 P.M.

Guided Bus Tours

See the zoo from the top of a double-decker bus. A tour guide tells about the animals while you see the sights.

Special Botanical Bus Tours show off the zoo's plants. These tours start in front of the orchid greenhouses at 2:00 P.M.

Ride the Skyfari

From 10:00 A.M. until 4:00 P.M., you can have a bird's-eye view from the Skyfari tram. Board near the entrance and travel over the treetops to the polar bears.

Exploring on Foot

Many wonders of the zoo can be enjoyed best by walking. Follow the path past the Flamingo Lagoon into Fern Canyon. Or stroll through the Petting Paddock to comb a goat or pet a sheep.

* All times are estimates. Check the zoo's Web site before visiting.

Feeding the Animals

You can watch the animals eat and see what foods they enjoy! On weekends, you can even help feed the giraffes.

Animal	Feeding Time*
Giraffes	12:00 noon and 5:00 P.M.
Apes	4:00 P.M.
Elephants	6:00 P.M.
Hippos	7:00 P.M

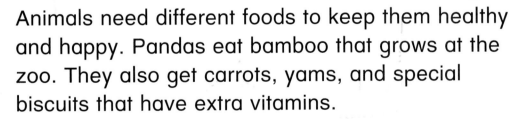

Animals need different foods to keep them healthy and happy. Pandas eat bamboo that grows at the zoo. They also get carrots, yams, and special biscuits that have extra vitamins.

Many animals like frozen treats. Lions get blocks of ice with meatballs inside. Clouded Leopards enjoy papaya frozen in blocks of ice.

Monkeys eat fruits and vegetables and like popcorn as a snack.

* These are estimated feeding times. Check the zoo's Web site before visiting.

San Diego Zoo's Wild Animal Park

The Wild Animal Park is 35 miles north of the San Diego Zoo. Many of the animals move freely in areas like their natural habitats.

Getting Around the Wild Animal Park

The Wgasa Bush Line Railroad

An electric train takes you on a 3-mile guided tour of the Asian and African field exhibits. See lions, tigers, zebras, and elephants in a natural setting.

Balloon Safari

Ride in a quiet helium balloon that takes off just west of the Lion Camp. Rise 400 feet in the air to see lions, rhinos, giraffes, wildebeests, and gazelles.

Photo Caravan Safari Tours

Get close to African and Asian animals on a 2-hour safari. The guide will stop the trucks so that you can take close-up photos of the animals.

Condor Ridge

At Condor Ridge, see California condors with wings that can measure more than 9 feet. They can fly as fast as 55 miles per hour and as high as 15,000 feet.

Frequent Flyers Bird Show

See more than 40 different kinds of birds, such as the East African Crowned Crane. Shows are at 12:00 noon, 2:00 P.M., and 4:00 P.M. daily.*

Elephant Show

Asian and African elephants can be seen from the park's Elephant Overlook. In the elephant show, the animals show off their strength and intelligence. Shows are at 1:00 P.M. and 3:00 P.M. every day.*

* Show times may change. Check with the zoo for exact times.

Everyday Mathematics®

CALIFORNIA

The University of Chicago School Mathematics Project

My Reference Book

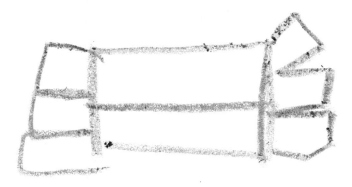

 Wright Group

The McGraw·Hill Companies

UCSMP Elementary Materials Component

Max Bell, Director, UCSMP Elementary Materials Component; Director, *Everyday Mathematics* First Edition
James McBride, Director, *Everyday Mathematics* Second Edition
Andy Isaacs, Director, *Everyday Mathematics* Third Edition
Amy Dillard, Associate Director, *Everyday Mathematics* Third Edition

Authors
Mary Ellen Dairyko, Rachel Malpass McCall,
Cheryl G. Moran

Technical Art
Diana Barrie

Technology Advisor
James Flanders

Contributors
Cynthia Annorh, Robert Hartfield, James McBride,
Cindy Pauletti, Kara Stalzer, Michael Wilson

www.WrightGroup.com

 **Wright Group**

Send all inquiries to:
Wright Group/McGraw-Hill
P.O. Box 812960
Chicago, IL 60681

ISBN   978-0-07-609789-0
MHID   0-07-609789-7

2 3 4 5 6 7 8 9 QWD 13 12 11 10 09 08 07

The **McGraw·Hill** Companies

Contents

Contents

Reference Frames   77

Estimation   91

Patterns and Functions   95

Mathematics... Every Day
Patterns All Around   103

Number Stories   107

Contents

Games   119

Calculators   159

Index   166

Dear Children,

A reference book is a book that helps people find information. Some other reference books are dictionaries, encyclopedias, and cookbooks. *My Reference Book* can help you find out more about the mathematics you learn in class. You can read this reference book with your teacher, your family, and your classmates.

You will find lots of math in this book.
Some of the things you will find are:

◆ counts

◆ shapes

◆ clocks

◆ money

◆ measures

◆ fractions

◆ graphs

◆ patterns

◆ number stories

◆ fact families

◆ math tools

◆ games

You will also find some big words. A grown-up can help you read these words. HI   HELLO   HEY

We hope you enjoy this book.

Sincerely,
The Authors

Numbers and Counting

Numbers All Around

Read It Together

Numbers are used in many ways.

Count the shells. How many are there?

- Numbers are used for **counting.**

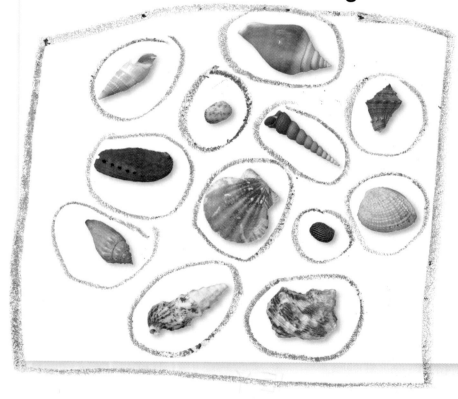

● Numbers are used as **measures.**

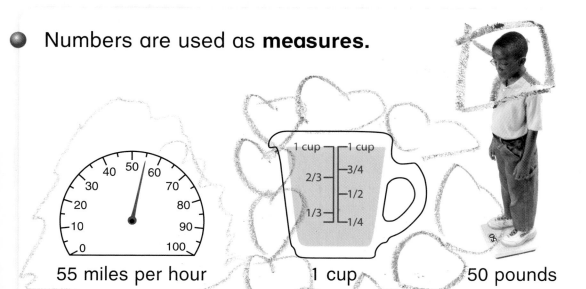

55 miles per hour   1 cup   50 pounds

● Numbers are used to **compare.**

Lily is 5 inches taller than Jake.

A nickel is worth $\frac{1}{2}$ as much as a dime.

three   **3**

Numbers are used as **codes.**

Jane Smith
2507 W. Sunnyside A
Eureka Springs, AR 72632

zip code

312-555-2794

bar code

area code
and phone number

What is **your** area code and phone number?

Numbers are used to **show locations.**

35

We live at
35 Park Street.

The football is on
the 50-yard line.

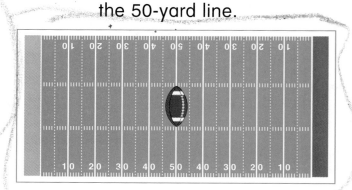

Numbers are used for **ordering.**

Note

When you use numbers, say what you are counting or measuring. That is called a "unit."

5 <u>**pennies**</u>

50 <u>**pounds**</u> ——— unit

5th <u>**child**</u>

Try It Together

Look around the room. Try to find numbers used in different ways.

Counting Tools

Read It Together

Number lines and **number grids** are tools for counting. To count on a **number line,** think about hopping from one number to another.

● Count by 2s. Start at 0.

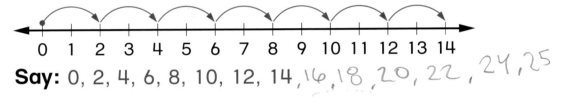

Say: 0, 2, 4, 6, 8, 10, 12, 14, 16, 18, 20, 22, 24, 25

Count back by 1s. Start at 10.

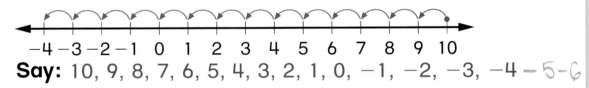

Say: 10, 9, 8, 7, 6, 5, 4, 3, 2, 1, 0, −1, −2, −3, −4 −5−6

Count by 5s. Start at 0.

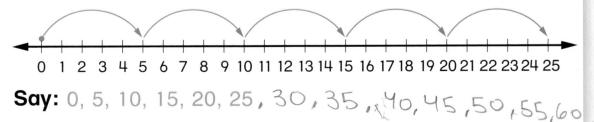

Say: 0, 5, 10, 15, 20, 25, 30, 35, 40, 45, 50, 55, 60

Numbers on a **number grid** are in rows and columns.

−9	−8	−7	−6	−5	−4	−3	−2	−1	0
1	2	3	4	5	6	7	8	9	10
11	12	13	14	15	16	17	18	19	20
21	22	23	24	25	26	27	28	29	30
31	32	33	34	35	36	37	38	39	40
41	42	43	44	45	46	47	48	49	50
51	52	53	54	55	56	57	58	59	60
61	62	63	64	65	66	67	68	69	70
71	72	73	74	75	76	77	78	79	80
81	82	83	84	85	86	87	88	89	90
91	92	93	94	95	96	97	98	99	100
101	102	103	104	105	106	107	108	109	110

Note

To move from row to row, follow the matching colors.

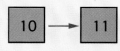

−9	−8	−7	−6	−5	−4	−3	−2	−1	0
1	2	3	4	5	6	7	8	9	10
11	12	13	14	15	16	17	18	19	20
21	22	23	24	25	26	27	28	29	30
31	32	33	34	35	36	37	38	39	40
41	42	43	44	45	46	47	48	49	50
51	52	53	54	55	56	57	58	59	60
61	62	63	64	65	66	67	68	69	70
71	72	73	74	75	76	77	78	79	80
81	82	83	84	85	86	87	88	89	90
91	92	93	94	95	96	97	98	99	100
101	102	103	104	105	106	107	108	109	110

● When you move to the right, numbers get *bigger* by 1. For example: 15 is 1 *more* than 14.

When you move to the left, numbers get *smaller* by 1. For example: 23 is 1 *less* than 24.

When you move down, numbers get *bigger* by 10. For example: 37 is 10 *more* than 27.

When you move up, numbers get *smaller* by 10. For example: 43 is 10 *less* than 53.

Comparing Numbers

Read It Together

We use symbols to **compare** numbers.

25 > 20
25 **is greater than** 20.

20 < 25
20 **is less than** 25.

Note

The symbol ≠ means **is not equal to.**

20 = 20
20 **is the same as** 20.
20 **is equal to** 20.

To help you remember what > and < mean, think about an alligator.

The alligator eats the larger number.

31 > 18

Place Value

Read It Together

Numbers can be written using these **digits.**

0 1 2 3 4 5 6 7 8 9

● The place of a digit in a number tells how much
the digit is worth.

thousands	,	hundreds	tens	ones
1	,	3	4	2

The **1** in the **thousands** place is worth **1,000.**
The **3** in the **hundreds** place is worth **300.**
The **4** in the **tens** place is worth **40.**
The **2** in the **ones** place is worth **2.**

1,234,567,89

The number shown is 1,342.
Say: One thousand, three hundred forty-two.

1,000 + 300 + 45
————————————
1345

Base-10 blocks can show numbers.

Base-10 block	Base-10 shorthand	Name	Value
▫	▪	cube	1
▯	|	long	10
▦	▢	flat	100
▨	◱	big cube	1,000

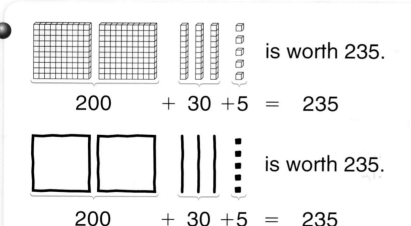

200   + 30 +5 = 235

is worth 235.

200   + 30 +5 = 235

is worth 235.

Try It Together

Use blocks to show 46 and 64. Is the 6 worth more in 46 or 64?

Fractions

A whole object can be divided into **equal parts.**

- a whole clock face
the clock face divided into 4 equal parts

- a whole cracker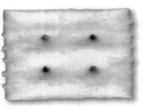
the cracker divided into 3 equal parts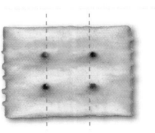

- a whole hexagon
the hexagon divided into 6 equal parts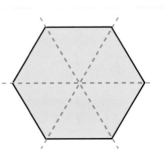

Fractions can name parts of a whole.

The whole clock face is divided into 4 equal parts.

1 part is shaded.

$\frac{1}{4}$ of the clock face is shaded.

$\frac{1}{4}$

1 ← **numerator** (number of shaded parts)

4 ← **denominator** (number of equal parts)

$\frac{1}{4}$ is a **unit fraction.**
A unit fraction has 1 in the numerator.

● The whole cracker is divided into 3 equal parts.

$\frac{1}{3}$ of the cracker has jelly.

$\frac{2}{3}$ of the cracker does not have jelly.

● The whole hexagon is divided into 6 equal parts.

$\frac{4}{6}$ of the hexagon is green.

$\frac{2}{6}$ of the hexagon is yellow.

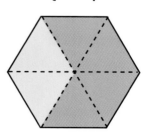

Fractions can name parts of a collection.

● a collection of 6 pennies

3 of the pennies show heads.
$\frac{3}{6}$ of the pennies show heads.

● a collection of 5 flowers

1 of the flowers is red.
$\left(\frac{1}{5}\right)$ of the flowers is red.

← **unit fraction**

Note

When the numerator and the denominator of a fraction are the same, the fraction means "1 whole."

$$\frac{4}{4} = 1$$

Equivalent fractions name the same amount.

 $\frac{1}{2}$ is shaded.

 $\frac{2}{4}$ is shaded.

$\frac{1}{2}$ is equivalent to $\frac{2}{4}$ because the same amount is shaded.

$$\frac{1}{2} = \frac{2}{4}$$

$\frac{2}{6}$ is equivalent to $\frac{1}{3}$.

$$\frac{2}{6} = \frac{1}{3}$$

Try It Together

Find a whole object divided into equal parts. What fraction names one part of the whole?

Name-Collection Box

Read It Together

A **name-collection box** is a place to write different names for the same number.

This tag
names the box.

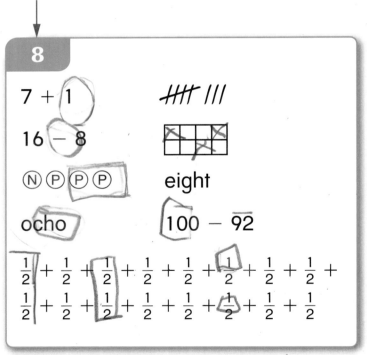

This is a name-collection box for 8.

Counting is an important part of our lives. People count every day.

◄ An umpire counts the number of strikes and balls pitched to each batter.

◀ Swimmers count their strokes so they know when to turn.

Herpetologists study reptiles and amphibians. They count the growth rings of box turtles to find out about how old they are. ▼

This is a growth ring.

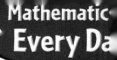

◄ Workers use machines to count the coins made each day at the U.S. Mint. How might you count 10,000 pennies?

Hematologists are blood specialists. They count red blood cells to see how healthy a person is. ▼

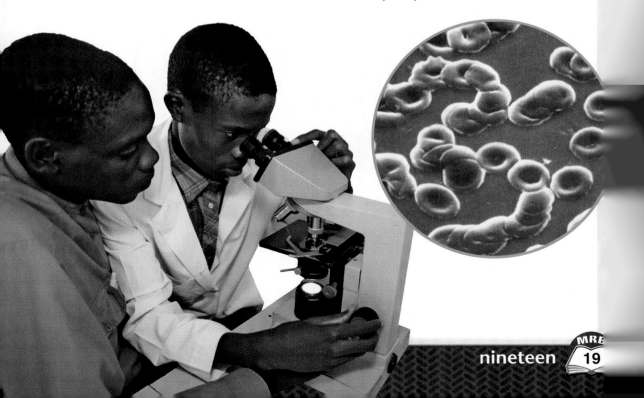

Wildlife researchers have to estimate the number of birds in a large flock. Why might wildlife researchers need to count birds? ▼

What things can *you* count?

Operations and Computation

Addition and Subtraction

Read It Together

We use words and symbols for addition
and subtraction.

- Use + to show addition.

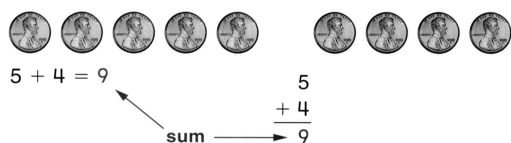

$5 + 4 = 9$

$$
\begin{array}{r}
5 \\
+\ 4 \\
\hline
9
\end{array}
$$

sum ⟶ 9

- Use − to show subtraction.

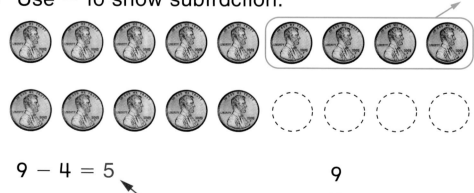

$9 - 4 = 5$

$$
\begin{array}{r}
9 \\
-\ 4 \\
\hline
5
\end{array}
$$

difference ⟶ 5

A **number line** can help you find sums.

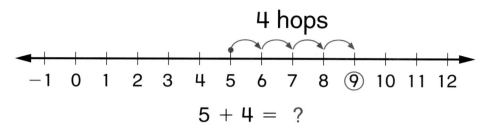

4 hops

$$5 + 4 = \ ?$$

1. Start at 5.
2. **Count up** 4 hops.
   Land on 9.

$$5 + 4 = 9$$

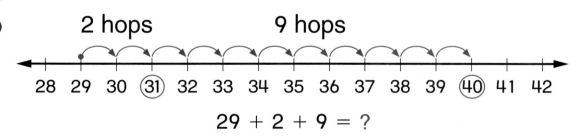

2 hops   9 hops

$$29 + 2 + 9 = \ ?$$

1. Start at 29.
2. **Count up** 2 hops.
   Land on 31.
3. **Count up** 9 more hops.
   Land on 40.

$$29 + 2 + 9 = 40$$

A number line can help you find differences.

● One way:

7 hops

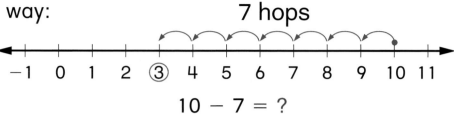

$$10 - 7 = ?$$

1. Start at 10.

2. **Count back** 7 hops. Land on 3.

$$10 - 7 = 3$$

● Another way:

? hops

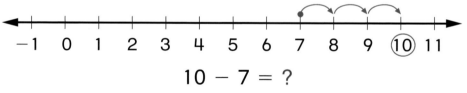

$$10 - 7 = ?$$

1. Start at 7.

Think: How many hops from 7 to 10?

2. **Count up** to 10. There are 3 hops.

$$10 - 7 = 3$$

Try It Together

Add and subtract numbers on a number line.

Fact Families

Read It Together

A **fact family** is a group of related facts that uses the same numbers.

Dominoes can help you find fact families.

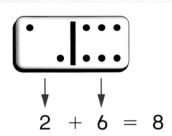

2 + 6 = 8

2 + 6 = 8	8 − 6 = 2
6 + 2 = 8	8 − 2 = 6

This is the fact family for 2, 6, and 8.

7 + 7 = 14

7 + 7 = 14   14 − 7 = 7

This **doubles fact family** uses 7, 7, and 14.

Note

Doubles fact families have only two facts instead of four.

You can use an **Addition/Subtraction Facts Table** to help you find fact families.

+,−	0	1	2	3	4	5	6	7	8	⑨	10
0	0	1	2	3	4	5	6	7	8	9	10
1	1	2	3	4	5	6	7	8	9	10	11
2	2	3	4	5	6	7	8	9	10	11	12
3	3	4	5	6	7	8	9	10	11	12	13
4	4	5	6	7	8	9	10	11	12	13	14
5	5	6	7	8	9	10	11	12	13	14	15
6	6	7	8	9	10	11	12	13	14	15	16
⑦	7	8	9	10	11	12	13	14	15	⑯	17
8	8	9	10	11	12	13	14	15	16	17	18
9	9	10	11	12	13	14	15	16	17	18	19
10	10	11	12	13	14	15	16	17	18	19	20

This is the fact family for 9, 7, and 16.

$9 + 7 = 16$ $16 - 7 = 9$

$7 + 9 = 16$ $16 - 9 = 7$

Fact triangles show the 3 numbers in a fact family.

$3 + 5 = 8 \qquad 8 - 5 = 3$
$5 + 3 = 8 \qquad 8 - 3 = 5$

This is the fact family
for 8, 5, and 3.

You can use fact triangles to practice facts.

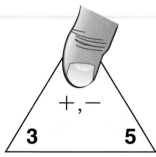

To practice addition, cover
the number by the dot.

Cover 8. Think:
$3 + 5 = ? \qquad 5 + 3 = ?$

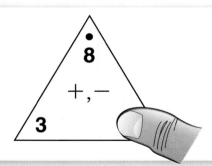

To practice subtraction, cover
one of the other numbers.

Cover 5. Think:
$8 - 3 = ? \qquad 3 + ? = 8$

Try It Together

Use your fact triangles to play *Beat the Calculator*.

Adding Larger Numbers

Read It Together

There are many different ways to add larger numbers.

Try this ⟶ 17 + 25 = ?

- You can use **base-10 blocks** to add.

  1. Show 17.

  2. Add 25 more.

  3. Count all the blocks. 30   12

  $$17 + 25 = 42$$

  How can you trade base-10 blocks to make counting easier?

You can use a **number grid** to add.

−9	−8	−7	−6	−5	−4	−3	−2	−1	0
1	2	3	4	5	6	7	8	9	10
11	12	13	14	15	16	17	18	19	20
21	22	23	24	25	26	27	28	29	30
31	32	33	34	35	36	37	38	39	40
41	42	43	44	45	46	47	48	49	50
51	52	53	54	55	56	57	58	59	60
61	62	63	64	65	66	67	68	69	70
71	72	73	74	75	76	77	78	79	80
81	82	83	84	85	86	87	88	89	90
91	92	93	94	95	96	97	98	99	100
101	102	103	104	105	106	107	108	109	110

Note

At the end of a row, go to the beginning of the next row and keep counting.

$$17 + 25 = ?$$

1. Start at 17.

2. Add 20.
   • Move down 2 rows to 37.

3. Add 5.
   • Count 5 more to 42.

$$17 + 25 = 42$$

● You can use the **partial-sums addition method** to add.

$$17 + 25 = ?$$

	10s	1s
	1	7
+	2	5
	3	0
	1	2
	4	2

1. Add the 10s. $10 + 20 =$

2. Add the 1s. $7 + 5 =$

3. Add the partial sums. $30 + 12 =$

$$17 + 25 = 42$$

● You can also use the **U.S. traditional addition method** to add.

$$17 + 25 = ?$$

1. Add the 1s.

$7 + 5 = 12$

- 12 is 1 ten and 2 ones.
- Write 1 above the numbers in the 10s place.
- Write 2 in the 1s place below the line.

```
      1
    1  7
+   2  5
_____
       2
```

2. Add the 10s.

$1 + 1 + 2 = 4$

- Write 4 in the 10s place below the line.

```
      1
    1  7
+   2  5
_____
    4  2
```

$$17 + 25 = 42$$

You can use the **U.S. traditional addition method** to add larger numbers too.

$$398 + 427 = ?$$

1. Add the 1s.   **8 + 7 = 15**
- 15 is 1 ten and 5 ones.
- Write 1 above the numbers in the 10s place.
- Write 5 in the 1s place below the line.

```
      1
    3 9 8
  + 4 2 7
  -------
        5
```

2. Add the 10s.   **1 + 9 + 2 = 12**
- 12 tens is 1 hundred and 2 tens.
- Write 1 above the numbers in the 100s place and 2 in the 10s place below the line.

```
    1 1
    3 9 8
  + 4 2 7
  -------
      2 5
```

3. Add the 100s.   **1 + 3 + 4 = 8**
- Write 8 in the 100s place below the line.

```
    1 1
    3 9 8
  + 4 2 7
  -------
    8 2 5
```

$$398 + 427 = 825$$

Try It Together

Add two larger numbers. Show a partner what you did.

MRB
30B

Subtracting Larger Numbers

There are many different ways to subtract larger numbers.

Try this ⟶ 43 − 27 = ?

● You can use **base-10 blocks** to subtract.

1. Show 43.

2. Take away 20.

3. Cannot take away 7.
Trade 1 long for 10 cubes.

4. Take away 7.

5. 1 long and 6 cubes are left.

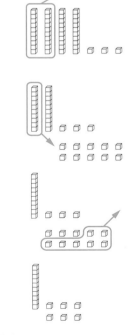

$$43 - 27 = 16$$

You can use a **number grid** to subtract.

−9	−8	−7	−6	−5	−4	−3	−2	−1	0
1	2	3	4	5	6	7	8	9	10
11	12	13	14	15	16	17	18	19	20
21	22	23	24	25	26	27	28	29	30
31	32	33	34	35	36	37	38	39	40
41	42	43	44	45	46	47	48	49	50
51	52	53	54	55	56	57	58	59	60
61	62	63	64	65	66	67	68	69	70
71	72	73	74	75	76	77	78	79	80
81	82	83	84	85	86	87	88	89	90
91	92	93	94	95	96	97	98	99	100
101	102	103	104	105	106	107	108	109	110

$$43 - 27 = ?$$

1. Start at 43.
2. Subtract 20.
   - Move up 2 rows to 23.
3. Subtract 7.
   - Count back 7 to 16.

$$43 - 27 = 16$$

Another way to subtract on a number grid is to count up.

−9	−8	−7	−6	−5	−4	−3	−2	−1	0
1	2	3	4	5	6	7	8	9	10
11	12	13	14	15	16	17	18	19	20
21	22	23	24	25	26	27	28	29	30
31	32	33	34	35	36	37	38	39	40
41	42	43	44	45	46	47	48	49	50
51	52	53	54	55	56	57	58	59	60
61	62	63	64	65	66	67	68	69	70
71	72	73	74	75	76	77	78	79	80
81	82	83	84	85	86	87	88	89	90
91	92	93	94	95	96	97	98	99	100
101	102	103	104	105	106	107	108	109	110

Note

You can count up to find how much change you get back at the store.

$$43 - 27 = ?$$

1. Start at 27.

2. Count up 10.
   • Move down 1 row to 37.

3. Count up 6 more.
   • Count 6 more to 43.

$$43 - 27 = 16$$

● You can use the **counting-up subtraction method** to subtract.

$$43 - 27 = ?$$

1. Start at 27.
   Count up to the nearest ten.

2. Count up by tens to 40.

3. Count up to 43.

$$
\begin{array}{r}
27 \\
+\ ③ \\
\hline
30 \\
+\ ⑩ \\
\hline
40 \\
+\ ③ \\
\hline
\mathbf{43}
\end{array}
$$

Circle each number that you count up.

4. Add the numbers you circled.

$$3 + 10 + 3 = 16$$

$$
\begin{array}{r}
3 \\
10 \\
+\ 3 \\
\hline
16
\end{array}
$$

Think:

$$
\begin{array}{ccccc}
& +3 & & +10 & & +3 \\
27 & \rightarrow & 30 & \rightarrow & 40 & \rightarrow & 43
\end{array}
$$

$$3 + 10 + 3 = 16$$

$$43 - 27 = 16$$

You can use the **trade-first subtraction method** to subtract 2-digit numbers.

$$43 - 27 = ?$$

You cannot take 7 ones from 3 ones without getting a negative number.

10s	1s
4	3
− 2	7

1. So trade 1 ten for 10 ones.
   4 tens − 1 ten = 3 tens
   3 ones + 10 ones = 13 ones

10s	1s
3	13
~~4~~	~~3~~
− 2	7

2. Subtract the tens and the ones.

10s	1s
3	13
~~4~~	~~3~~
− 2	7
1	6

$$43 - 27 = 16$$

Why can you trade 10 ones for 1 ten?

You can also use the **trade-first subtraction method** to subtract numbers larger than two digits.

$$352 - 168 = ?$$

1. Look at the 1s place.
You cannot take 8 ones from 2 ones without getting a negative number.

100s	10s	1s
3	5	2
− 1	6	8

2. So trade 1 ten for 10 ones.
5 tens − 1 ten = 4 tens
2 ones + 10 ones = 12 ones

100s	10s	1s
	4	12
3	5̶	2̶
− 1	6	8

3. Look at the 10s place. You cannot take 6 tens from 4 tens without getting a negative number.

100s	10s	1s
	4	12
3	5̶	2̶
− 1	6	8

MRB
35A

4. So trade 1 hundred for 10 tens.
3 hundreds − 1 hundred = 2 hundreds
4 tens + 10 tens = 14 tens

100s	10s	1s
	14	
2	~~4~~	12
~~3~~	~~5~~	~~2~~
− 1	6	8

5. Now subtract the hundreds,
the tens, and the ones.

100s	10s	1s
	14	
2	~~4~~	12
~~3~~	~~5~~	~~2~~
− 1	6	8
1	8	4

$$352 - 168 = 184$$

Try It Together

Subtract two larger numbers. Show a partner what you did.

Equal Groups and Equal Shares

Read It Together

Equal groups have the same number of things.

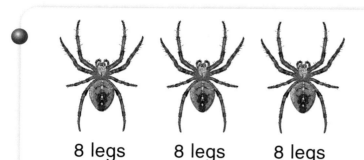

8 legs   8 legs   8 legs

There are three spiders.
Each spider has 8 legs.
There are 24 legs in all.

Sometimes you have things that you want to share equally.

When you make **equal shares,** each group has the same number of objects.

There are 4 boys.
The boys share 12 marbles equally.
Each boy gets 3 marbles.
They have **equal shares.**

Multiplication and Division Fact Triangles

Read It Together

Multiplication and division **fact triangles** show the 3 numbers in a fact family.

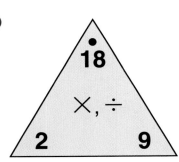

$2 \times 9 = 18 \qquad 18 \div 9 = 2$
$9 \times 2 = 18 \qquad 18 \div 2 = 9$

This is the fact family for 2, 9, and 18.

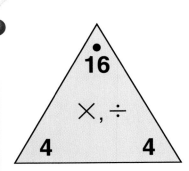

$4 \times 4 = 16 \qquad 16 \div 4 = 4$

This is the fact family for 4, 4, and 16.

You can use fact triangles to practice facts.

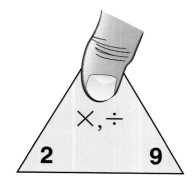

To practice multiplication, cover the number by the dot.

Cover 18. Think:

$2 \times 9 = ?$ $9 \times 2 = ?$

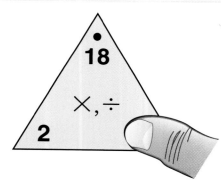

To practice division, cover one of the other numbers.

Cover 9. Think:

$18 \div 2 = ?$ $2 \times ? = 18$

Try It Together

Use your multiplication and division fact triangles to play *Beat the Calculator*.

Data and Chance

Tally Chart and Line Plot

Read It Together

Information someone has collected is called **data.**

● A **tally chart** is one way to organize data.

Teeth Lost in Mr. Alan's Class

Number of Teeth Lost	Number of Children
0	//////
1	////// //
2	///
3	////
4	/
5	

Note

Remember: Every fifth tally mark goes across a group of four tally marks.

//////

This tally chart shows the number of teeth lost by the children in Mr. Alan's class.

There are 3 tally marks to the right of 2. This means that 3 children lost 2 teeth.

● A **line plot** is another way to organize data.

Teeth Lost in Mr. Alan's Class

```
                    X
                    X
Number        X     X
  of          X     X           X
Children      X     X     X     X
              X     X     X     X
              X     X     X     X     X
          ─────────────────────────────────
              0     1     2     3     4     5
                 Number of Teeth Lost
```

This line plot shows the same data as the tally chart on page 40.

There are 3 Xs above 2.

This means that 3 children lost 2 teeth.

How many teeth have you lost?

Try It Together

How many children did not lose any teeth?

Graphs

Read It Together

A **picture graph** uses a picture or a symbol to show data.

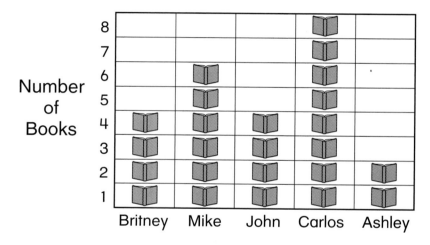

Books Read in Ms. Cook's Class

Number of Books

There are 4 📖 above Britney.
This means that Britney read 4 books.

There are 6 📖 above Mike.
This means that Mike read 6 books.

Mike read more books than Britney.

A **pictograph** also uses pictures or symbols to show data.

The **key** on a pictograph tells what each picture stands for.

Books Read in Ms. Cook's Class

Britney	📖 📖
Mike	📖 📖 📖
John	📖 📖
Carlos	📖 📖 📖 📖
Ashley	📖

Key: Each 📖 = 2 books.

This pictograph shows the same data as the picture graph on page 42.

The key on this pictograph tells us that each 📖 stands for 2 books read.

There are 2 📖 to the right of Britney. This means that Britney read 4 books.

There are 3 📖 to the right of Mike. This means that Mike read 6 books.

Carlos read the most books.

A **bar graph** uses bars to show data.

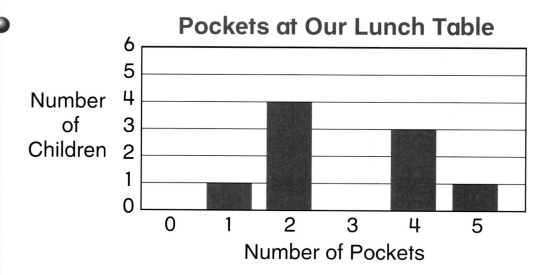

Pockets at Our Lunch Table

Number of Children

Number of Pockets

The bar above 5 shows that 1 child has 5 pockets.

The bar above 4 is taller. This shows that more children have 4 pockets than 5 pockets.

There is no bar above 3. This shows that no children have 3 pockets.

Try It Together

How many children are at the lunch table?

Describing Data

Read It Together

Here are some numbers that describe data.

● The **mode** is the number that occurs most often.
The mode of pockets at the lunch table is **2.**
More children have 2 pockets than any other number
of pockets.

The **maximum** is the largest number.
The maximum number of pockets at the lunch table is **5.**
One child has 5 pockets.

The **minimum** is the smallest number.
The minimum number of pockets at the lunch table is **1.**
One child has 1 pocket.

The **range** is the difference between the largest and
smallest numbers. Subtract the minimum from the
maximum to find the **range.**

maximum	5 pockets
minimum	− 1 pocket
range	**4 pockets**

The range of the number of pockets is **4.**

● The **median** is the middle number of a data set.

Pockets at Our Lunch Table

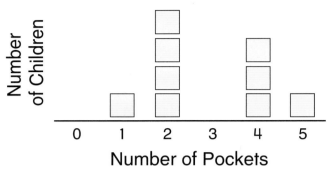

To find the **median:**

1. Put the number of pockets in order from the smallest number to the largest number.

1   2   2   2   2   4   4   4   5

2. Find the middle number of pockets.

1   2   2   2   **2**   4   4   4   5

⌐The middle number is the median.

The median number of pockets is **2.**

Try It Together

Ask 5 people how many pockets they have. Organize the data you collect. Then find the mode, range, and median.

Chance

Read It Together

When you spin a color spinner, you might spin any of the colors. You can **predict** what color you will spin, but you might be wrong.

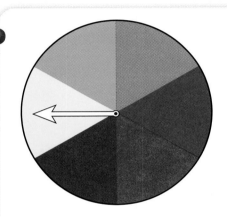

The spinner has an **equal chance** of landing on yellow, green, orange, blue, red, or purple.

The spinner has **no chance** of landing on pink because there is no pink on the spinner.

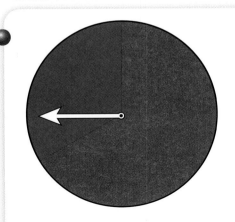

It is **certain** that the spinner will land on either red or blue.

The chance of landing on red is greater than the chance of landing on blue.

What is most likely to happen?

- Suppose you close your eyes, reach in the bag, and grab a block.

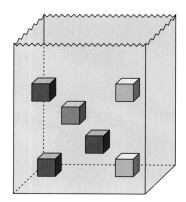

3 red blocks
2 yellow blocks
1 blue block

You are **most likely** to grab a red block because there are more red than either blue or yellow blocks.

You are **least likely** to grab a blue block because there are fewer blue than either red or yellow blocks.

Try It Together

Put 1 red crayon, 2 yellow crayons, and 3 blue crayons in a bag. Which crayon are you most likely to grab? Which crayon are you least likely to grab? Then close your eyes, reach in the bag, and grab a crayon. What might happen if you did it again? What if you did it 10 times? 100 times?

Geometry

Points, Line Segments, and Lines

Read It Together

A **point** is a location in space.
A point is like a dot.
We show a point like this: •A
It is called point A.

Line segments and **lines** are made of points.

Shape	Name of Shape	Symbol for Shape
endpoints C D	This is a **line segment.** It has 2 **endpoints.** It is called line segment CD or line segment DC.	$\overline{CD}$ or $\overline{DC}$
F E	This is a **line.** It is called line EF or line FE. The arrowheads show that the line goes on and on in both directions.	$\overleftrightarrow{EF}$ or $\overleftrightarrow{FE}$

Parallel lines never meet. They are always the same distance apart.

Parallel line segments are parts of parallel lines.

These lines are parallel.

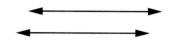

These line segments are parallel.

These lines are not parallel.
They **intersect.**

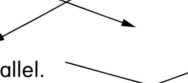

These line segments are not parallel.
They **intersect.**

Try It Together

Look around the room. Find as many parallel line segments as you can.

2-Dimensional Shapes

A plane shape is flat. Plane shapes are also called **2-dimensional.** You can draw them on paper.

- This 2-dimensional shape is a **polygon.** Polygons are made of line segments.

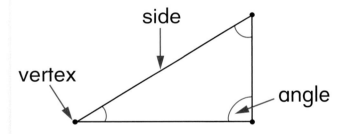

side

vertex

angle

Note

A point where two sides meet is called a **vertex.** The plural of *vertex* is *vertices*.

This polygon has 3 **sides,** 3 **angles,** and 3 **vertices.**

- These 2-dimensional shapes are also polygons.

These 2-dimensional shapes are polygons.

These 2-dimensional shapes are **not** polygons.

The sides cross.   Some sides are curved.

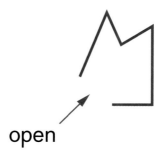

There are not 3
or more sides.

open

The sides are not closed.

Note

All polygons are closed shapes
but not all closed shapes
are polygons.

Here are more 2-dimensional shapes.

A **circle** has no straight sides.

A **triangle** has 3 sides.

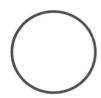

A **pentagon** has 5 sides.

A **hexagon** has 6 sides.

A **heptagon** has 7 sides.

An **octagon** has 8 sides.

Which shape has 2 more sides than a triangle?

These 2-dimensional shapes are all **quadrangles.**
Quadrangles are also called **quadrilaterals.**

● A quadrangle has 4 sides, 4 angles, and 4 vertices.

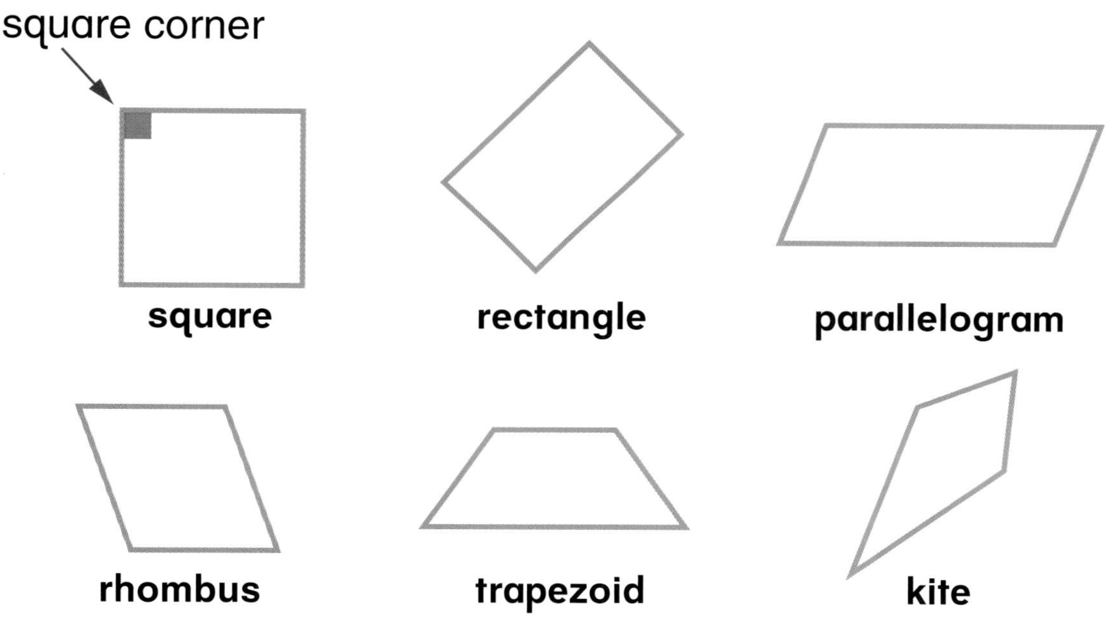

square corner

square

rectangle

parallelogram

rhombus

trapezoid

kite

Try It Together

Choose one of the 2-dimensional shapes on pages 54–55.
Describe it to a partner without saying the shape's name.
Can your partner tell what shape you are describing?

3-Dimensional Shapes

A **3-dimensional** shape takes up space.
Objects you hold are 3-dimensional.

- Some 3-dimensional shapes are **rectangular prisms.**

 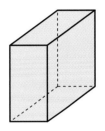  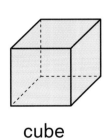

cube   cube

- Some 3-dimensional shapes are **pyramids.**

apex

 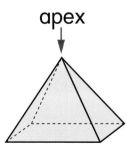 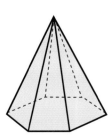

Some 3-dimensional shapes are **cones.**

apex

Some 3-dimensional shapes are **cylinders.**

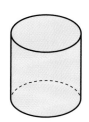

Some 3-dimensional shapes are **spheres.**

• Some 3-dimensional shapes have faces, edges, and vertices.

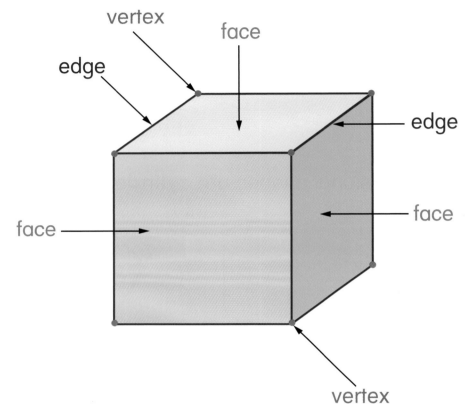

vertex

face

edge

edge

face

face

vertex

A cube has 6 **faces**, 12 **edges**, and 8 **vertices**.

Some of the faces on some 3-dimensional shapes are called **bases.**

● The bases are shaded green.

cone

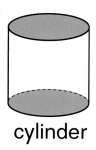

cylinder

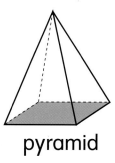

pyramid

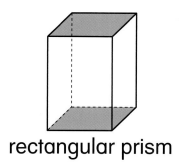

rectangular prism

Try It Together

Look around the room. Find 3-dimensional shapes.
Can you find a rectangular prism? Can you find a sphere?

Line Symmetry

Read It Together

A shape has **line symmetry** if you can
fold it in half and both halves match exactly.
The fold line is called the **line of symmetry.**

● The parts match.

line of symmetry

The parts do not match.

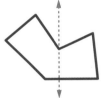

not a line of symmetry

● 2 lines of symmetry

4 lines of symmetry

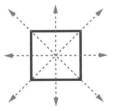

Try It Together

How many lines of symmetry does a circle have?

Measurement

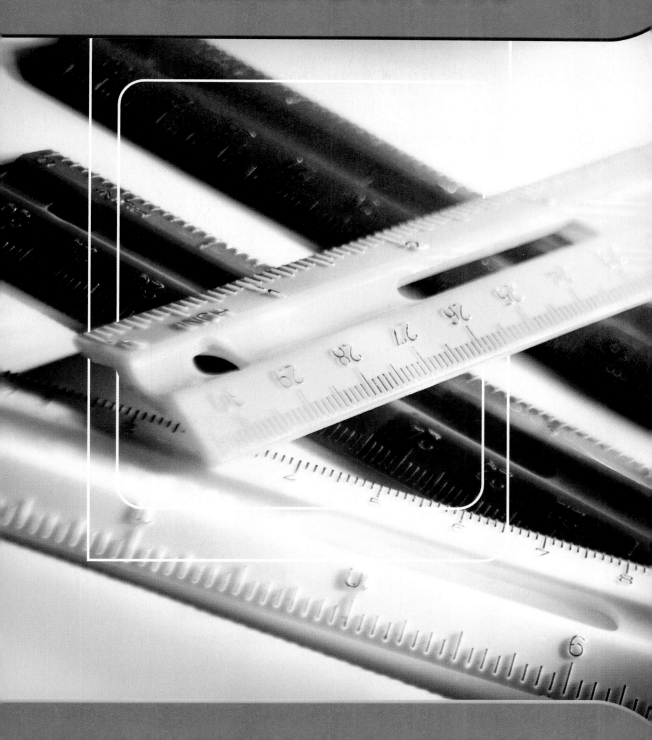

Length

You can use parts of your body to measure. Body measures tell us about how long something is. These measures are different for different people.

Here are some examples.

digit

The eraser is about 4 digits long.

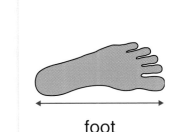

foot

The door is about 5 feet wide.

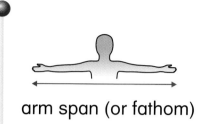

arm span (or fathom)

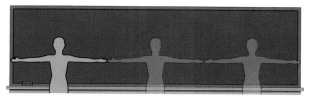

The chalkboard is about
3 arm spans wide.

Here are some more examples.

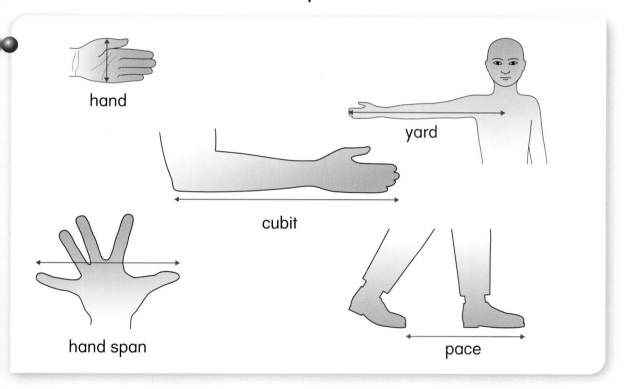

hand

yard

cubit

hand span

pace

Did You Know?

Digit is another name
for a finger or a toe.

How many digits do
you have?

sixty-three **63**

● You can use **tools** to measure length.
These tools use **standard units** that never change.
Standard units are the same for everyone.

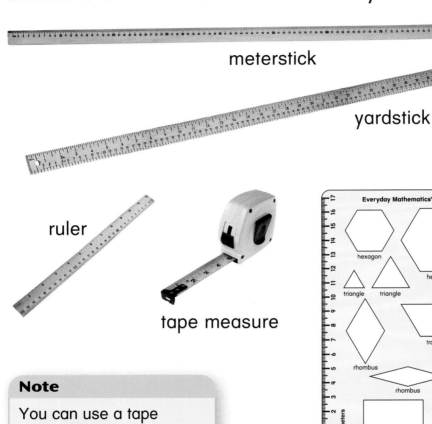

meterstick

yardstick

ruler

tape measure

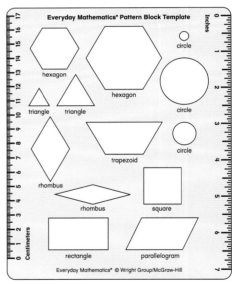

Pattern-Block Template

Note

You can use a tape measure to measure the distance around objects. We call this distance the **circumference.**

An **inch** is one standard unit.

Rulers are often marked with inches on one edge.

Measure to the nearest inch.

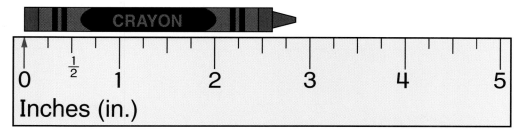

The crayon is **about 3 inches** long.

Note

When you measure, line up one end of the object with the 0-mark on the ruler.

Measure to the nearest $\frac{1}{2}$ inch.

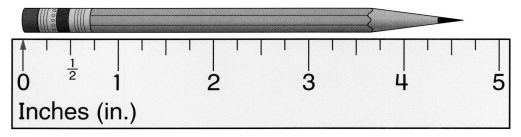

The pencil is **about 4 $\frac{1}{2}$ inches** long.

A **centimeter** is another standard unit.

Rulers are often marked with centimeters on one edge.

● Measure to the nearest centimeter.

The paper clip is **about 5 centimeters** long.

● Measure to the nearest $\frac{1}{2}$ centimeter.

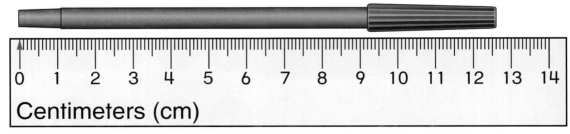

The marker is **about $12\frac{1}{2}$ centimeters** long.

Today, people use two different measurement systems. One is the U.S. customary system, and the other is the metric system.

Here are some **units of length.**

Tables of Measures of Length

U.S. Customary Units	Metric Units
1 yard (yd) = 36 inches (in.) = 3 feet (ft)	1 meter (m) = 100 centimeters (cm) = 10 decimeters (dm)
1 foot = 12 inches = $\frac{1}{3}$ yard	1 decimeter = 10 centimeters = $\frac{1}{10}$ meter
1 inch = $\frac{1}{12}$ foot = $\frac{1}{36}$ yard	1 centimeter = $\frac{1}{10}$ decimeter = $\frac{1}{100}$ meter

Try It Together

Estimate the length of an object. Then measure it with a ruler.

Perimeter and Area

Read It Together

What are some ways you use measurement?

- Sometimes you want to know the distance around a shape. This distance is the **perimeter** of the shape.

- Add the lengths of the sides to find the perimeter.

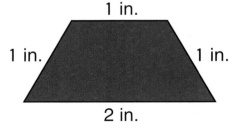

1 in.

1 in.   1 in.

2 in.

2 in. + 1 in. + 1 in. + 1 in. = 5 in.

The perimeter of the shape is 5 inches.

Sometimes you want to know the amount of surface inside a shape. This amount of surface inside a shape is the **area** of the shape.

Count the squares to find the area.

				1
			2	3
		4	5	6
	7	8	9	10
11	12	13	14	15

Note

Use *square* units for the area of a shape.

Each square is 1 square centimeter.

The area of the shape is 15 square centimeters.

Try It Together

Draw a shape that has a perimeter of 10 inches.
Compare your shape with a partner's shape.

Capacity and Weight

Read It Together

The amount a container can hold is called its **capacity.**

- You can use these tools to measure capacity.

measuring cup

measuring spoons

What could you use a measuring cup for?

graduated cylinder

5-gallon bucket

Weight is the measure of how heavy something is.

● You can use these tools to measure weight.

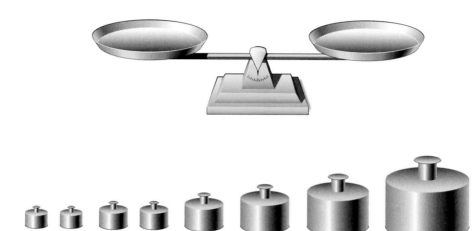

1g   1g   2g   2g   5g   10g   20g   50g

balance scale with weight set

bath scale

spring scale

Here are some **units of capacity.**

Tables of Measures of Capacity

U.S. Customary Units	Metric Units
1 cup (c) = $\frac{1}{2}$ pint 1 pint (pt) = 2 cups 1 quart (qt) = 2 pints 1 quart = 4 cups 1 gallon (gal) = 4 quarts 1 half-gallon ($\frac{1}{2}$ gal) = 2 quarts	1 liter (L) = 1,000 milliliters (mL) $\frac{1}{2}$ liter = 500 milliliters

Here are some **units of weight.**

Tables of Measures of Weight

U.S. Customary Units	Metric Units
1 pound (lb) = 16 ounces (oz) 1 ton (T) = 2,000 pounds	1 kilogram (kg) = 1,000 grams (g) 1 metric ton (t) = 1,000 kilograms

Try It Together

How many cups are in a gallon?

Measures All Around: Animals and Tools

Have you ever wondered how large animals are measured? What about tiny animals or dangerous animals? People use many different tools to measure animals.

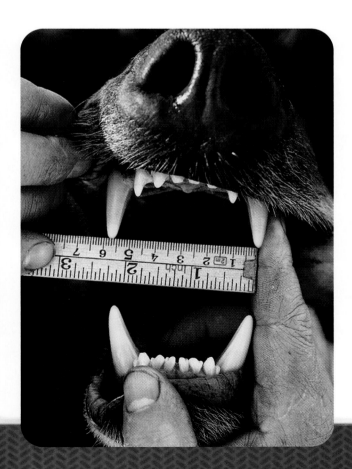

◄ A bear researcher uses a ruler to measure the distance between a bear's canine teeth.

These scientists use calipers to measure the length of a sea turtle's shell and the length of a large egg. A caliper measures things from end to end. ➤

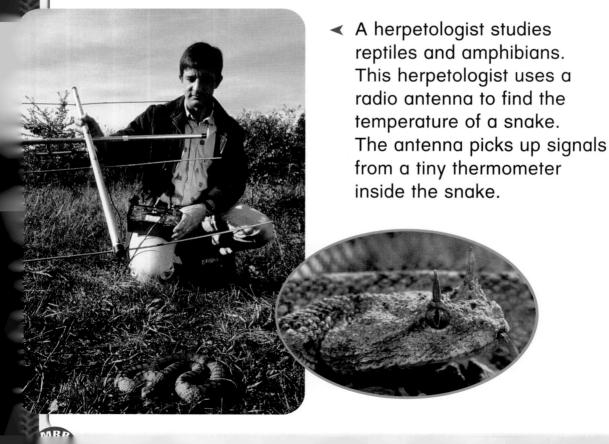

◄ A herpetologist studies reptiles and amphibians. This herpetologist uses a radio antenna to find the temperature of a snake. The antenna picks up signals from a tiny thermometer inside the snake.

◄ An ornithologist studies birds. This ornithologist uses a spring scale to weigh an albatross chick.

This ornithologist uses a special thermometer to measure the surface temperature of a penguin. ➤

These zookeepers use a large platform scale to weigh elephants. What other animals might need an extra-large scale? ➤

MRE

A zookeeper uses a digital scale to weigh a leopard cub. This scale measures weight in grams. Why might zookeepers want to know the weight of a young animal? ▼

What tools do *you* use to measure?

Reference Frames

Time

Read It Together

There are many ways to show **time.** One way uses hour and minute hands and numbers to show time. Another way uses only numbers.

- You can use analog clocks and analog watches to show time.

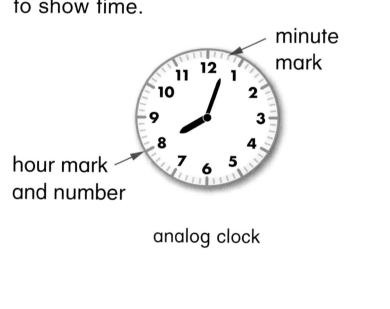

minute mark

hour mark and number

analog clock

analog watch

Read the hour numbers on the clock.

You can use digital clocks and digital watches to show time.

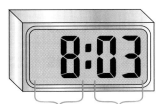

hour : minutes

digital clock

digital watch

Did You Know?

The first clock with a minute hand was invented in 1577.

The digital clock was invented in 1956.

The **hour hand** shows the hour.

The hour hand is usually the shorter hand on a clock face.

clockwise

hour mark

hour number

hour hand

The hour hand takes 1 hour to move from an hour mark to the next hour mark.

It is **almost** 3 o'clock.

It is **between** 8 o'clock and 9 o'clock.

It is **a little after** 5 o'clock.

The **minute hand** shows the minutes.

The minute hand is usually the longer hand on a clock face.

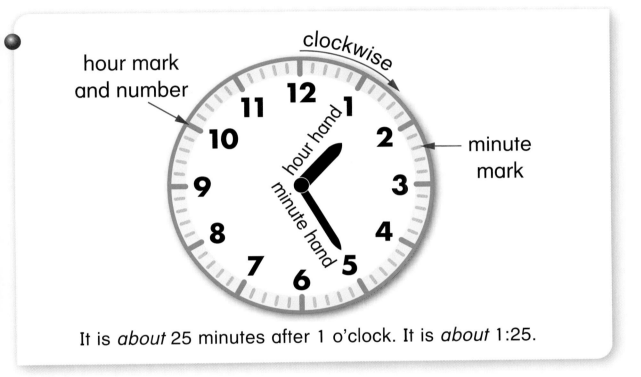

It is *about* 25 minutes after 1 o'clock. It is *about* 1:25.

The minute hand takes 1 minute to move from a minute mark to the next minute mark.

All hands on a clock move **clockwise.**

● The hours from midnight to noon are **A.M.** hours.

12:00 A.M.
12 midnight

7:30 A.M.
half past 7

10:15 A.M.
a quarter after 10

12:00 P.M.
12 noon

The hours from noon to midnight are **P.M.** hours.

12:00 P.M.
12 noon

3:30 P.M.
half past 3

7:45 P.M.
a quarter to 8

12:00 A.M.
12 midnight

Calendars

Read It Together

We use a **calendar** to keep track of the days of the week and the months in a year.

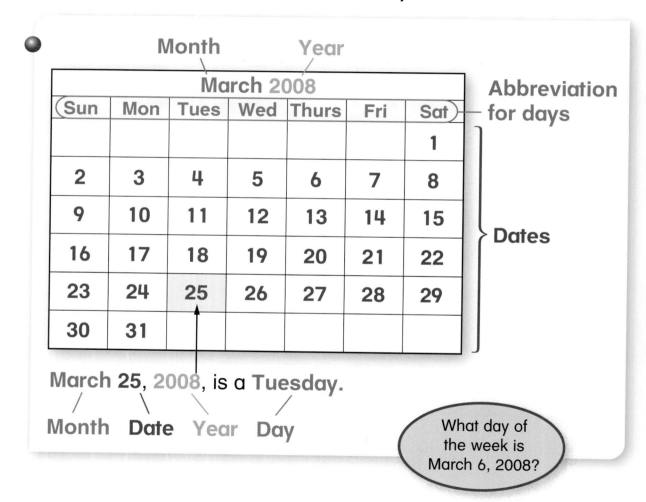

Month   Year

			March 2008				Abbreviation for days
Sun	Mon	Tues	Wed	Thurs	Fri	Sat
						1
2	3	4	5	6	7	8
9	10	11	12	13	14	15
16	17	18	19	20	21	22
23	24	25	26	27	28	29
30	31					

Dates

March **25**, 2008, is a **Tuesday**.

Month Date Year Day

What day of the week is March 6, 2008?

Every month has 30 or 31 days, except for one month.

Which month does not have 30 or 31 days?

Number of Days in Each Month

January	31 days	July	31 days
February	28 or 29* days	August	31 days
March	31 days	September	30 days
April	30 days	October	31 days
May	31 days	November	30 days
June	30 days	December	31 days
* 29 days in leap years			

There is a **leap year** almost every four years.

We add an extra day to February in a leap year.

Did You Know?

It takes about $365\frac{1}{4}$ days for the Earth to make one complete trip around the sun. This is why we add a day almost every four years.

Here are some **units of time.**

Units of Time

1 minute = 60 seconds
1 hour = 60 minutes
1 day = 24 hours
1 week = 7 days
1 month = 28, 29, 30, or 31 days
1 year = 12 months
1 year = 52 weeks plus 1 day, or 52 weeks plus 2 days (in leap year)
1 year = 365 days, or 366 days (in leap year)
1 decade = 10 years
1 century = 100 years
1 millennium = 1,000 years

Try It Together

How many days are in 3 weeks? In 5 weeks?

Temperature

We use a **thermometer** to tell the **temperature.**

Temperature tells how hot or cold something is.

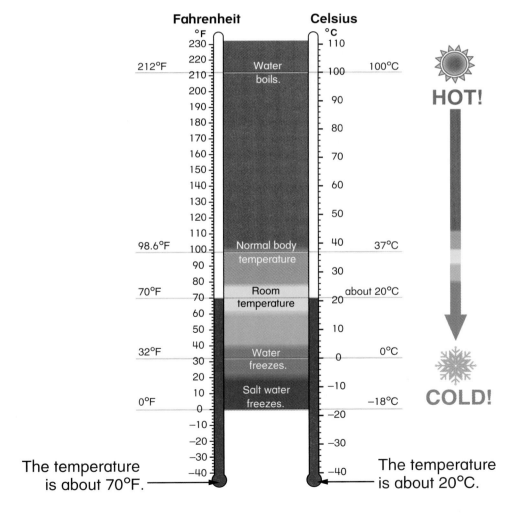

The temperature is about 70°F.

The temperature is about 20°C.

Money

Read It Together

We use **money** to buy things.

Here are some of the coins and bills used in the United States.

	Penny 1¢ $0.01	Nickel 5¢ $0.05
Heads or Front		
Tails or Back		
Equivalencies	1 Ⓟ	1 Ⓝ 5 Ⓟ

How many nickels make 3 dollars?

Dime 10¢ $0.10	Quarter 25¢ $0.25	Dollar 100¢ $1.00

1 Ⓓ 2 Ⓝ 10 Ⓟ	1 Ⓠ 5 Ⓝ 25 Ⓟ	1 $1 4 Ⓠ 10 Ⓓ 20 Ⓝ 100 Ⓟ

You can use **dollars-and-cents notation** to write money amounts.

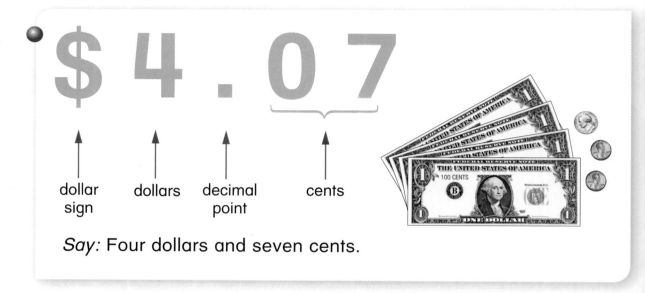

$4.07

dollar sign | dollars | decimal point | cents

Say: Four dollars and seven cents.

You can use symbols to show money amounts.

$1 $1 $1 $1   (N)   (P)   (P)

Try It Together

Play "Coin Exchange" on pages 128 and 129 or "One-Dollar Exchange" on pages 144 and 145.

Estimation

Estimation

An **estimate** is an answer that should be close to an exact answer. Sometimes an estimate is called a **ballpark estimate.** We can use ballpark estimates—estimates that are "close enough"—to check answers.

You make estimates every day. When you say the word *about* before a number, you are making an estimate.

One way to estimate a large number of objects is to look at a smaller part.

● About how many cubes are in the jar?

There are about 25 cubes on the top layer and 6 layers of cubes in the jar. Four 25s is 100 and two 25s is 50. 100 plus 50 equals 150.

There are about 150 cubes in the jar.

Another way to find an estimate is to change numbers to **close-but-easier** numbers.

- There are 100 cartons of milk in the lunchroom.
  53 first graders need milk.
  38 second graders need milk.
  Is there enough milk in the lunchroom for the first and second graders?

  Close-but-easier
  numbers

  $$53 \longrightarrow 50$$
  $$38 \longrightarrow + 40$$
  $$\overline{ 90}$$

  About 90 cartons of milk are needed.
  So 100 cartons is enough for all
  of the first and second graders.

What word lets someone know you are making an estimate?

Use an estimate to check if an answer makes sense.

● Anna's class checked out 94 library books last month.
37 books were returned.
How many books are still checked out?

Add up to find the answer.

$$+3 \quad +50 \quad +4$$
$$37 \rightarrow 40 \rightarrow 90 \rightarrow 94$$

$$3 + 50 + 4 = 57$$

57 books are still checked out.

Estimate to check the answer.

Close-but-easier
numbers

$$94 \longrightarrow 90$$
$$37 \longrightarrow -40$$
$$\overline{50}$$

Since 50 is close to 57, the answer makes sense.

Patterns and Functions

Patterns

Read It Together

Shapes can make **patterns.** You can tell what comes next in a pattern if you know the rule.

- Some patterns repeat over and over.

Numbers can also make patterns.

- Even numbers and odd numbers can make dot patterns.

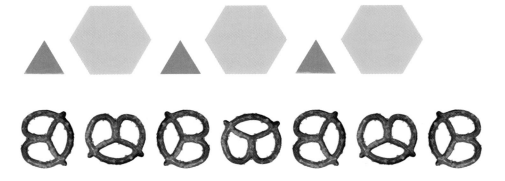

Even Numbers				Odd Numbers			
2	4	6	8	1	3	5	7

A number grid has many patterns.

● This number grid shows odd and even numbers.

-9	-8	-7	-6	-5	-4	-3	-2	-1	0
1	2	3	4	5	6	7	8	9	10
11	12	13	14	15	16	17	18	19	20
21	22	23	24	25	26	27	28	29	30
31	32	33	34	35	36	37	38	39	40
41	42	43	44	45	46	47	48	49	50
51	52	53	54	55	56	57	58	59	60
61	62	63	64	65	66	67	68	69	70
71	72	73	74	75	76	77	78	79	80
81	82	83	84	85	86	87	88	89	90
91	92	93	94	95	96	97	98	99	100
101	102	103	104	105	106	107	108	109	110

The **odd** numbers are green.
The **even** numbers are orange.

Try It Together

Look at these numbers. 203, 205, 207, 209, ...
Tell a partner the number that comes next.

Frames and Arrows

Read It Together

In a **Frames-and-Arrows diagram,** the **frames** are the shapes that hold the numbers, and the **arrows** show the path from one frame to the next.

Each diagram has a **rule box.** The **rule** in the box tells how to get from one frame to the next.

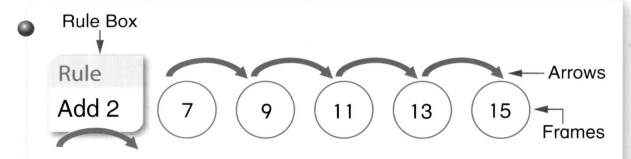

Rule Box

Rule
Add 2   7   9   11   13   15 ← Arrows
Frames

◆ The rule is **Add 2.**

◆ Add 2 to 7. That's 9. 9 is in the second frame.
   Add 2 to 9. That's 11. 11 is in the third frame.

Why is 15 in the last frame?

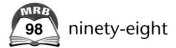

● Use the rule to find the missing number.

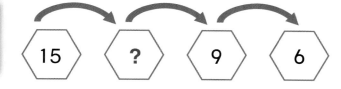

Rule
Subtract 3

15 ? 9 6

◆ The rule is **Subtract 3.**
   15 − 3 = **12**
   12 is the missing number.

● Use the numbers in the frames to find the rule.

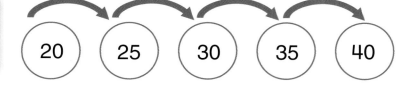

Rule
?

20 25 30 35 40

◆ Each number is **5** more
   than the number before it.
   The rule is **Add 5.**

Note

Another name for this
rule is **Count up 5.**

Function Machines

Read It Together

A **function machine** uses a rule to change numbers. You put a number into the machine. The machine uses the rule to change the number. The changed number comes out of the machine.

◆ If you put 2 into the machine, it will **add 10** to 2.
  The number 12 will come out.

◆ If you put 4 into the machine, it will **add 10** to 4.
  The number 14 will come out.

◆ If you put 0 into the machine, it will **add 10** to 0. The number 10 will come out.

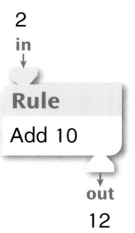

2
in

Rule

Add 10

out
12

An **In and Out** table keeps track of how a function machine changes numbers.

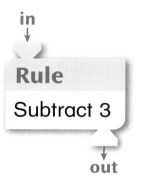

in	out
4	1
5	2
6	3
7	4

Write the numbers that are put into the machine in the **in** column. Write the numbers that come out of the machine in the **out** column.

◆ If you put 4 into the machine, the machine subtracts 3 from 4. 1 comes out.

◆ If 2 comes out, then 5 was put in. The machine subtracted 3 from 5.

Use the in and out numbers to find a rule for a function machine.

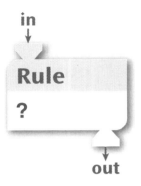

in	out
2	0
5	3
6	4
9	7

◆ How do you get from 2 to 0? **Subtract 2.**
How do you get from 5 to 3? **Subtract 2.**
Can you **subtract 2** to get from 6 to 4? Yes.

◆ The rule is **Subtract 2.**

Try It Together

Ask your partner to write a rule. Write an In and Out table for the rule.

Patterns All Around

Patterns are everywhere! You can see patterns in nature. You can see patterns in the things people make.

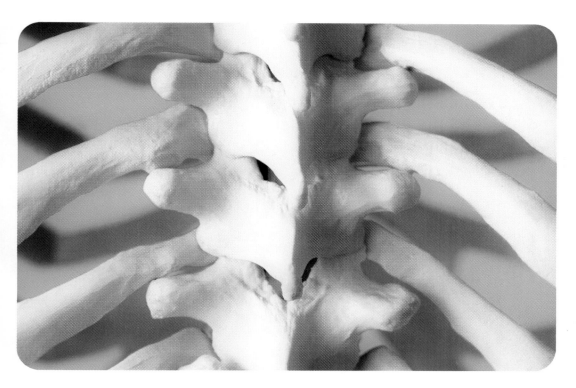

▲ What patterns do you see in the human spine and ribs?

◄ Corn and kiwi
seeds grow in
patterns. ▼

Describe the patterns you
see on the inside and outside
of nautilus shells. ▼

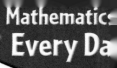

◄ What patterns do you
see in this cloth?

Hula dancers make patterns
when they dance together. ▼

▲ Pueblo Indians
paint patterns
like these on
their pottery.

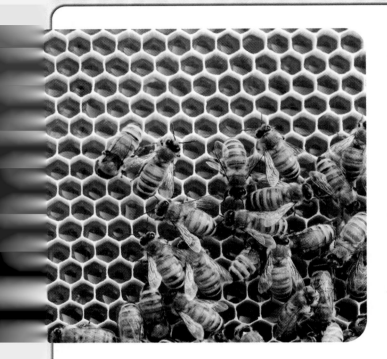

◄ You can see patterns in the honeycomb made by bees.

900
+ 1000
1900

What patterns do you see in this spiral staircase? ➤

Look around. What patterns can you find in nature? What patterns can you find that are made by people?

Number Stories

Number Stories and Situation Diagrams

Read It Together

Number stories are stories that use numbers. One way to solve number stories is to use diagrams.

Some number stories are about a total and its parts. You can use a **parts-and-total diagram** to help you solve them.

● There are 8 yellow crayons and 6 blue crayons. How many crayons are there in all?

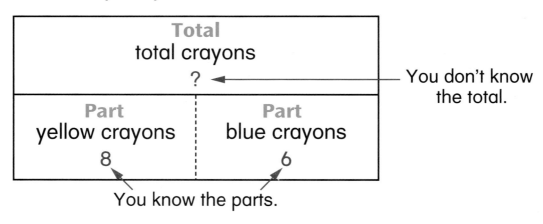

Total
total crayons
? ← You don't know the total.

Part	Part
yellow crayons	blue crayons
8	6

You know the parts.

Add the parts to find the total.
Number model: 8 + 6 = **14**
There are **14** crayons in all.

Sometimes you need to find one of the parts.

● There are 24 children on a bus.
9 children are girls. How many children are boys?

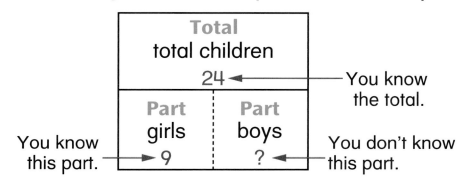

You can subtract to solve the problem.
Subtract the part you know from the total.
The answer is the other part.
Number model: 24 − 9 = **15**   **15** boys on the bus

● You can also add up to solve the problem.
Start with the part you know. Add up to the total.
The amount you add up is the other part.

$$+1 \qquad +10 \qquad +4$$
$$9 \longrightarrow 10 \longrightarrow 20 \longrightarrow 24$$

1 + 10 + 4 = **15**
Number model: 9 + **15** = 24   **15** boys on the bus

Some number stories are about comparisons. You can use a **comparison diagram** to help you solve them.

● Jim is 13 years old. Ron is 9 years old.
How many years older is Jim than Ron?

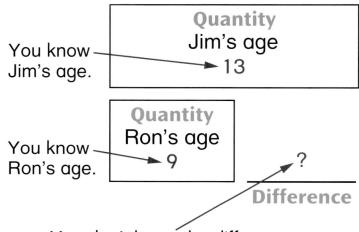

You know Jim's age.

Quantity
Jim's age
▶ 13

You know Ron's age.

Quantity
Ron's age
▶ 9

?

Difference

You don't know the difference between Jim's and Ron's ages.

You can subtract to find the difference.
Start with the larger number.
Subtract the smaller number.
The answer is the difference.

Number model: $13 - 9 = \mathbf{4}$

Jim is **4** years older than Ron.

You can also add up to find the difference.
Start with the smaller number.
Add up to the larger number.
The amount you add up is the difference.

$$9 \xrightarrow{+1} 10 \xrightarrow{+3} 13$$

$1 + 3 = \mathbf{4}$

Number model: $9 + \mathbf{4} = 13$

Jim is **4** years older than Ron.

Tell your partner
a comparison
number story.

You can use a diagram to help you solve a number story about groups with equal numbers of objects.

● Mia has 4 packs of gum.
There are 5 sticks of gum in each pack.
How many sticks of gum are there in all?

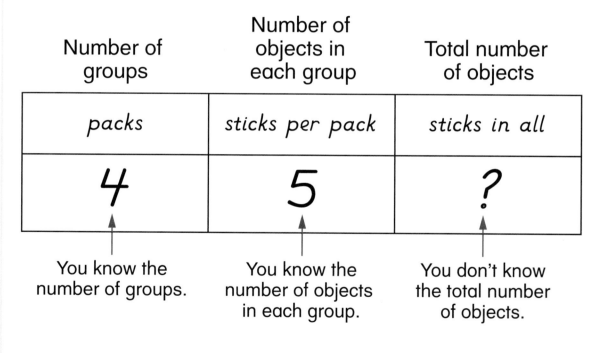

Number of groups	Number of objects in each group	Total number of objects
packs	*sticks per pack*	*sticks in all*
4	5	?

You know the number of groups.   You know the number of objects in each group.   You don't know the total number of objects.

Number model: 4 × 5 = **?**

There are many ways to solve the problem.

- You can draw a picture.

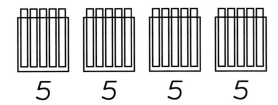

  5   5   5   5

- You can skip count by 5s.

  5, 10, 15, **20**

- You can add 5 four times.

  5 + 5 + 5 + 5 = **20**

Number model: $4 \times 5 = $ **20**

There are **20** sticks of gum in all.

Equal shares number stories are about dividing groups of objects into parts called **shares**. You can use a diagram to help you solve an equal share story.

● There are 24 marbles and 3 children.
Each child should get the same number of marbles.
How many marbles should each child get?

Number of shares	Number of objects in each share	Total number of objects
children	marbles per child	marbles in all
3	?	24

↑	↑	↑
You know the number of shares.	You don't know the number of objects in each share.	You know the total number of objects.

Number models: $3 \times ? = 24$

$$24 \div 3 = ?$$

● One way to solve the problem is to draw a picture.

● Another way is to use counters. Deal out 24 counters among 3 equal shares to see how many counters are in each share.

Number models: $3 \times 8 = 24$

$$24 \div 3 = 8$$

Each child has **8** marbles.

In change stories, the number you start with changes to more or changes to less. You can use a **change diagram** to help you solve a change-to-more story.

● Britney had 7 shells.
She found 9 more shells.
How many shells does Britney have in all?

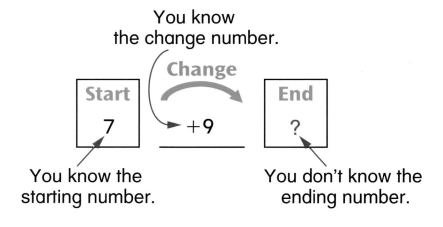

You know
the change number.

Change

Start
7

End
?

+9

You know the
starting number.

You don't know the
ending number.

Number model: 7 + 9 = **16**

Britney has **16** shells in all.

You can use a change diagram to help you solve a change-to-less story.

● There are 15 children on a bus.
6 children get off the bus.
How many children are left on the bus?

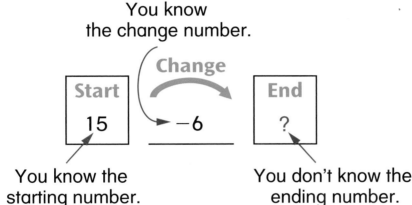

You know
the change number.

Change

Start
15

End
?

−6

You know the
starting number.

You don't know the
ending number.

Number model: 15 − 6 = **9**

There are **9** children left on the bus.

Sometimes you need to find the change in a change story. You can use a change diagram to help you solve this kind of number story.

● The morning temperature was 50°F.
The afternoon temperature was 63°F.
What was the temperature change?

You don't know
the change number.

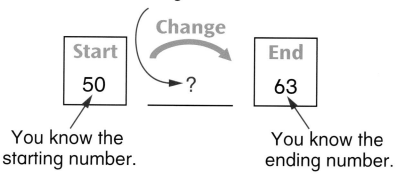

You know the
starting number.

You know the
ending number.

Number model: 50 + **13** = 63

The temperature change was +**13**°F.

Try It Together

Take turns with a partner making up and solving number stories.

Games

Addition Spin

Materials
- ❏ 1 *Addition Spin* spinner
- ❏ 1 paper clip
- ❏ 1 pencil
- ❏ 1 calculator
- ❏ 2 sheets of paper

Players 2

Skill Mental addition

Object of the game To have the larger total.

Directions

1. Players take turns being the "Spinner" and the "Checker."

2. The Spinner uses a pencil and a paper clip to make a spinner.

3. The Spinner spins the paper clip.

4. The Spinner writes the number that the paper clip points to. If the paper clip points to more than one number, the Spinner writes the smaller number.

5. The Spinner spins a second time and writes the new number.

6. The Spinner adds the 2 numbers and writes the sum. The Checker checks the sum of the 2 numbers by using a calculator.

7. If the sum is correct, the Spinner circles it. If the sum is incorrect, the Spinner corrects it but does not circle it.

8. Players switch roles. They stop after they have each played 5 turns. Each player uses a calculator to find the total of his or her circled scores.

9. The player with the larger total wins.

● Sam spins 5 and 25. He writes 30.
Mia spins 10 and 10. She writes 20.
Sam has the larger sum.

Addition Top-It

Materials ☐ number cards 0–10 (4 of each)

Players 2 to 4

Skill Addition facts 0 to 10

Object of the game To collect the most cards.

Directions

1. Shuffle the cards. Place the deck number-side down on the table.

2. Each player turns over 2 cards and calls out the sum of the numbers.

3. The player with the largest sum wins the round and takes all the cards.

4. In case of a tie for the largest sum, each tied player turns over 2 more cards and calls out the sum of the numbers. The player with the largest sum then takes all the cards from both plays.

5. The game ends when not enough cards are left for each player to have another turn.

6. The player with the most cards wins.

Andrew turns over a 2 and a 3. He says,
"2 plus 3 equals 5."

Tanya turns over an 8 and a 9. She says,
"8 plus 9 equals 17. 17 is more than 5.
I take all four cards."

Another Way to Play

Use dominoes instead of cards.

Beat the Calculator

Materials ☐ number cards 0–9
(4 of each)
☐ 1 calculator

Players 3

Skill Mental addition

Object of the game To add numbers faster than a player using a calculator.

Directions

1. One player is the "Caller." A second player is the "Calculator." The third player is the "Brain."

2. Shuffle the cards. Place the deck number-side down on the table.

3. The Caller draws 2 cards from the number deck and asks for the sum of the numbers.

4. The Calculator solves the problem *with* a calculator. The Brain solves it *without* a calculator. The Caller decides who got the answer first.

5. The caller continues to draw 2 cards at a time from the number deck and to ask for the sum of the numbers.

6. Players trade roles every 10 turns or so.

● The Caller draws a 2 and a 9. The Caller says, "2 plus 9."

The Brain and the Calculator each solve the problem.

The Caller decides who got the answer first.

Another Way to Play

The Caller can choose problems from the Facts Table.

Before and After

Materials ❑ number cards 0–10 (4 of each)

Players   2

Skill   Identifying numbers that are 1 less or 1 more than a given number

Object of the game To have fewer cards.

Directions

1. Shuffle the cards.

2. Deal 6 cards to each player.

3. Place 2 cards number-side up on the table.

4. Put the rest of the deck number-side down.

5. Players take turns. When it is your turn:
   • Look for any number in your hand that comes *before* or *after* one of the numbers on the table. Put it on top of the number. Play as many cards as you can.
   • Take as many cards as you need from the deck so that you have 6 cards again.

- If you can't play any cards when it is your turn, take 2 cards from the deck. Place them number-side up on top of the 2 numbers on the table. Try to play cards from your hand again. If you still can't, your turn is over.

6. The game is over when:
   - All cards have been taken from the deck.
   - No one can play any more cards.

7. The player holding fewer cards wins.

Sally gives 6 cards to Ricky and 6 cards to herself. Then she turns over a 9 card and a 2 card and places them on the table.

Ricky puts an 8 card on top of the 9 card and says, "8 is before 9." Then Ricky takes another card from the deck.

8 is before 9.

Coin Exchange

Materials ❏ 20 pennies, 10 nickels,
10 dimes, 2 quarters
❏ 2 six-sided dice
❏ 1 sheet of paper labeled "Bank"

Players   2

Skill   Coin equivalencies

Object of the game To have more money.

Directions

1. Place all of the coins in the "Bank."

2. Players take turns. When it is your turn, roll both dice and collect from the bank the amount shown on the dice.

3. Whenever you can:
- Exchange 5 pennies for a nickel in the bank.
- Exchange 2 nickels, or 5 pennies and 1 nickel, for a dime.
- Exchange a combination of nickels and dimes for a quarter.

4. The game ends when there are no more quarters in the bank.

5. The player with more money wins.

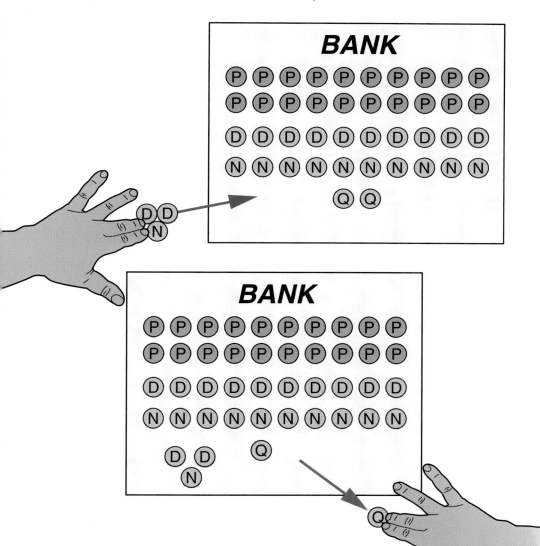

2 dimes and 1 nickel is the same as 1 quarter.

Difference Game

Materials ❏ number cards 1–10 (4 of each)
❏ 40 pennies
❏ 1 sheet of paper labeled "Bank"

Players   2

Skill   Subtraction facts

Object of the game To take more pennies.

Directions

1. Shuffle the cards. Place the deck number-side down on the table.

2. Put 40 pennies in the bank.

3. To play a round, each player:
  • Takes 1 card from the top of the deck.
  • Takes the same number of pennies from the bank as the number shown on their card.

4. Find out how many more pennies one player has than the other. Pair as many pennies as you can.

5. The player with more pennies keeps the extra pennies. The rest of the pennies go back into the bank.

6. The game is over when there are not enough pennies in the bank to play another round.

7. The player with more pennies wins the game.

Amy draws an 8. She takes 8 pennies from the bank.

John draws a 5. He takes 5 pennies from the bank.

Amy and John pair as many pennies as they can.

Amy has 3 more pennies than John. She keeps the 3 extra pennies and returns 5 of her pennies to the bank. John returns his 5 pennies to the bank.

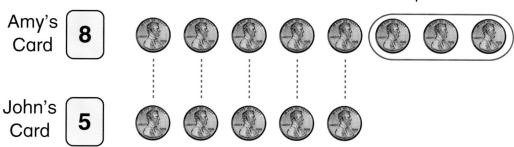

Amy keeps the difference – 3 pennies.

Amy's Card **8**

John's Card **5**

The Digit Game

Materials ❑ number cards
0–9 (4 of each)

Players   2

Skill   Making and comparing numbers

Object of the game To collect more cards.

Directions

1. Shuffle the cards. Place the deck number-side down on the table.

2. Each player draws 2 cards from the deck and uses them to make the larger 2-digit number.

3. The player with the larger number takes all 4 cards.

4. The game is over when all of the cards have been used.

5. The player with more cards wins.

Tina draws a 5 and a 3. She makes the number 53.
Raul draws a 1 and a 4. He makes the number 41.

Tina	**Raul**
Tina's cards are a 5 and a 3.	Raul's cards are a 1 and a 4.
5 3	1 4
Tina makes the number 53.	Raul makes the number 41.

Tina's number is larger than Raul's number.
Tina takes all 4 cards.

Other Ways to Play

Make 3-Digit Numbers: Each player draws 3 cards
and uses them to make the largest 3-digit number
possible. Play continues as in the regular game.

Fewer Cards Win: The player with fewer cards wins.

Fact Extension Game

Materials
- ❑ number cards 0–9 (4 of each)
- ❑ 1 six-sided die
- ❑ 1 calculator
- ❑ 1 sheet of paper for each player

Players 2

Skill Finding sums of 2-digit numbers and multiples of 10

Object of the game To have the higher total.

Directions

1. Shuffle the cards. Place the deck number-side down on the table.

2. Each player draws 2 cards from the deck and makes the larger 2-digit number.

3. Players take turns rolling the die and making another 2-digit number by using the number on the die in the tens place and a zero in the ones place.

4. Each player adds his or her 2 numbers and records the sum on a sheet of paper.

5. After 4 rounds, players use a calculator to find the total of their 4 sums.

6. The player with the higher total wins.

Anna draws a 3 and a 5. She makes the number 53. Then Anna rolls a 6. She makes the number 60.

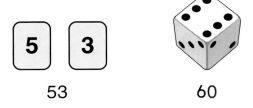

53   60

Anna finds the sum of her numbers.

53 + 60 = 113

Hit the Target

Materials   ❏ 1 calculator
              ❏ 1 *Hit the Target* Record Sheet
                 for each player

Players   2

Skill   Finding differences between 2-digit numbers and multiples of ten

Object of the game To reach the target number.

Directions

1. Players agree on a 2-digit multiple of 10 as a *target number*. Each player records the target number on a Record Sheet.

2. Player 1 selects a *starting number* less than the target number and records it on Player 2's Record Sheet.

3. Player 2 enters the starting number into the calculator and tries to change the starting number to the target number by adding or subtracting on the calculator.

4. Player 2 continues adding or subtracting until the target number is reached.

5. Player 1 records each change and its result on Player 2's Record Sheet.

6. Players switch roles. Player 2 selects a starting number for Player 1. Player 2 fills in Player 1's Record Sheet as Player 1 operates the calculator.

7. The player who reaches the target number in fewer tries wins the round.

Hit the Target **Record Sheet**

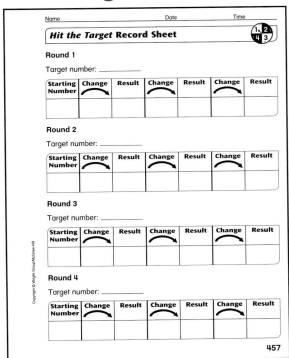

Name that Number

Materials ❏ number cards 0–20 (4 of each card 0–10, and 1 of each card 11–20)

Players 2 to 4 (the game is more fun when played by 3 or 4 players)

Skill Using addition and subtraction to name equivalent numbers

Object of the game To collect the most cards.

Directions

1. Shuffle the deck and place 5 cards number-side up on the table. Leave the rest of the deck number-side down. Then turn over the top card of the deck and lay it down next to the deck. The number on this card is the number to be named. Call this number the *target number*.

2. Players take turns. When it is your turn:
   • Try to name the target number by adding or subtracting the numbers on 2 or more of the 5 cards that are number-side up. A card may be used only once for each turn.

- If you can name the target number, take the cards you used to name it. Also take the target-number card. Then replace all the cards you took by drawing from the top of the deck.
- If you cannot name the target number, your turn is over. Turn over the top card of the deck and lay it down on the target-number pile. The number on this card is the new target number.

3. Play continues until all of the cards in the deck have been turned over. The player who has taken the most cards wins.

Mae and Joe take turns.

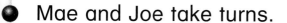

It is Mae's turn. The target number is 6.
Mae names the number with $12 - 4 - 2$.
She also could have said $4 + 2$ or $8 - 2$.

Mae takes the 12, 4, 2, and 6 cards. Then she replaces them by drawing cards from the deck.

Now it is Joe's turn.

Number-Grid Difference

Materials
- ❏ number cards 0–9 (4 of each)
- ❏ 1 completed number grid
- ❏ 1 *Number-Grid Difference* Record Sheet
- ❏ 2 counters
- ❏ 1 calculator

Players 2

Skill Subtraction of 2-digit numbers using the number grid

Object of the game To have the lower sum.

Directions

1. Shuffle the cards. Place the deck number-side down on the table.

2. Take turns. When it is your turn:
   - Take 2 cards from the deck and use them to make a 2-digit number. Place a counter on the grid to mark your number.
   - Find the difference between your number and your partner's number.
   - This difference is your score for the turn. Write the 2 numbers and your score on the Record Sheet.

3. Continue playing until each player has taken 5 turns and recorded 5 scores.

4. Find the sum of your 5 scores. You may use a calculator to add.

5. The player with the lower sum wins the game.

Ellie draws two 4s. She makes the number 44 and records it as her number on the Record Sheet.

Carlos draws a 6 and a 3 and makes the number 63. Ellie records 63 on the Record Sheet. Then Ellie subtracts.

$$63 - 44 = 19$$

Ellie records 19 as the difference.

Number Grid Difference **Record Sheet**

Number-Grid Game

Materials
- ❏ 1 number grid
- ❏ 1 six-sided die
- ❏ 1 game marker for each player

Players 2 or more

Skill Counting on the number grid

Object of the game To land on 110 with an exact roll.

Roll	Spaces
⚀	1 or 10
⚁	2 or 20
⚂	3
⚃	4
⚄	5
⚅	6

Directions

1. Players put their markers at 0 on the number grid.

2. Take turns. When it is your turn:
- Roll the die.
- Use the table to see how many spaces to move your marker.
- Move your marker that many spaces.

3. Continue playing. The winner is the first player to land on 110 with an exact roll.

Number Grid

-9	-8	-7	-6	-5	-4	-3	-2	-1	0
1	2	3	4	5	6	7	8	9	10
11	12	13	14	15	16	17	18	19	20
21	22	23	24	25	26	27	28	29	30
31	32	33	34	35	36	37	38	39	40
41	42	43	44	45	46	47	48	49	50
51	52	53	54	55	56	57	58	59	60
61	62	63	64	65	66	67	68	69	70
71	72	73	74	75	76	77	78	79	80
81	82	83	84	85	86	87	88	89	90
91	92	93	94	95	96	97	98	99	100
101	102	103	104	105	106	107	108	109	110

One-Dollar Exchange

Materials ❏ 1 dollar, 20 dimes, 20 pennies
❏ 1 Place-Value Mat per player
❏ 2 six-sided dice
❏ 1 sheet of paper labeled "Bank"

Players   2

Skill   Coin and bill equivalencies

Object of the game To make the exchange for a dollar.

Directions

1. Place all of the money in the "Bank."

2. Players take turns. When it is your turn:
- Roll the dice and find the total number of dots.
- Take that number of cents from the bank and place the coins on the Place-Value Mat.
- If there are 10 or more pennies in the Pennies column, exchange 10 pennies for 1 dime. Place the dime in the Dimes column.
- If there are 10 or more dimes in the Dimes column, exchange 10 dimes for 1 dollar.

3. The winner is the first player to make the
exchange for a dollar.

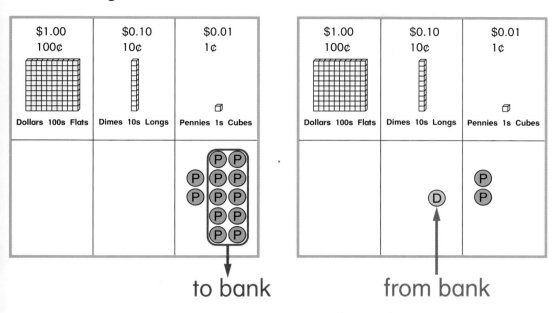

to bank   from bank

Exchanging 10 pennies for 1 dime

Penny Plate

Materials ❑ 10 pennies
❑ 1 small plastic plate

Players 2

Skill Sum-equals-ten facts

Object of the game To get 5 points.

Directions

1. Player 1:
   • Turns the plate upside-down.
   • Hides some of the pennies under the plate.
   • Puts the remaining pennies on top of the plate.

2. Player 2:

- Counts the pennies on top of the plate.
- Figures out how many pennies are hidden under the plate.

I see 6 pennies.
There are 10 pennies in all.
So there are 4 pennies
under the plate.

3. If the number is correct, Player 2 gets a point.

4. Players trade roles and repeat Steps 1 and 2.

5. Each player keeps a tally of their points.
The first player to get 5 points is the winner.

Another Way to Play

Use a different number of pennies.

Subtraction Top-It

Materials ❑ number cards 0–10 (4 of each)

Players 2 to 4

Skill Subtraction facts 0 to 10

Object of the game To collect the most cards.

Directions

1. Shuffle the cards. Place the deck number-side down on the table.

2. Each player turns over 2 cards and subtracts the smaller number from the larger number.

3. The player with the largest difference wins the round and takes all the cards.

4. In case of a tie for the largest difference, each tied player turns over 2 more cards and calls out the difference of the numbers. The player with the largest difference then takes all the cards from both plays.

5. The game ends when not enough cards are left for each player to have another turn.

6. The player with the most cards wins.

Ari turns over a 7 and a 5. He says,
"7 minus 5 equals 2."
Lola turns over a 9 and a 6. She says,
"9 minus 6 equals 3. 3 is more than 2.
I take all four cards."

Another Way to Play

Use dominoes instead of cards.

3, 2, 1 Game

Materials ❏ 1 sheet of paper
❏ 1 pencil for each player

Players 2

Skill Mental subtraction skills

Object of the game To reach exactly 0.

Directions

1. Write 21 at the top of the sheet of paper.

2. Players take turns. When it is your turn, subtract 1, 2, or 3 from the last number written on the paper.

3. The first player who subtracts and gets 0 as the answer wins the game.

21
−2
―――
19
−3
―――
16
−3
―――
13
−1
―――
12

Start with 21.
Player 1 subtracts 2.

Player 2 subtracts 3.

Player 1 subtracts 3.

Player 2 subtracts 1.

Each player has taken 2 turns.
The game continues until a player
subtracts and gets 0 as the answer.

Time Match

Materials ❑ 12 *Time Match* analog clock cards
❑ 12 *Time Match* digital clock cards

Players   2 or 3

Skill   Telling time

Object of the game To match the most cards.

Directions

1. Shuffle the cards. Place all 24 cards clock-side down on the table in a 4-by-6 array.

2. Players take turns. When it is your turn:
   • Turn over 2 cards.
   • If the cards match, take them. Your turn is over.
   • If the cards don't match, turn them back over so that they are clock-side down again in the same position. Your turn is over.

3. When all of the cards have been collected, the player with the most matches wins.

John turned over 2 cards. They both show 3:00. The cards match, so John took them.

Yoko turned over 2 cards. One card shows 6:00. The other card shows 5:15. The cards do not match, so Yoko will turn them back over so that they are clock-side down again in the same position.

These are John's cards.

Yoko turned over these cards. She will not take them.

Top-It

Materials ❑ number cards 0–10 (4 of each)

Players   2

Skill   Comparing numbers

Object of the game To collect more cards.

Directions

1. Shuffle the cards. Place the deck number-side down on the table.

2. Each player turns over 1 card and says the number on it.

3. The player with the larger number takes both cards. If both cards show the same number, each player turns over another card. The player with the larger number then takes all 4 cards for that round.

4. The game is over when all of the cards have been turned over.

5. The player with more cards wins.

Pam turns over a 4. She says, "4."

Mark turns over a 6. He says, "6.
6 is larger than 4, so I take both cards."

Another Way to Play

Use dominoes instead of cards.

Tric-Trac

Materials ❏ 2 six-sided dice
              ❏ 20 pennies
              ❏ 1 *Tric-Trac* Game Mat for each player

Players　2

Skill　Addition facts 0-10

Object of the game To have the lower sum.

Directions

1. Cover the empty circles on your game mat with pennies.

2. Take turns. When it is your turn:
   - Roll the dice. Find the total number of dots. This is your sum.
   - Move 1 of your pennies and cover your sum on your game mat.

OR

   - Move 2 or more of your pennies and cover any numbers that can be added together to equal your sum.

3. Play continues until no more numbers can be covered on your game mat. Your partner may continue playing, even after you are finished.

4. The game is over when neither player can cover any more numbers on his or her game mat.

5. Find the sum of your uncovered numbers. The player with the lower sum wins.

Set-up *Tric-Trac* Game Mat

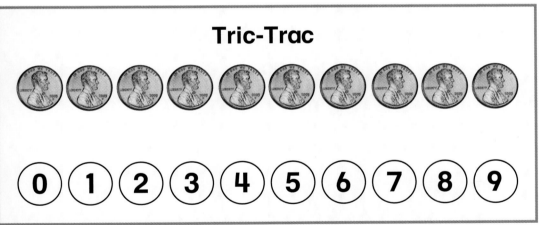

Turn to page 158 to see an example.

David rolled a 1 and a 2.
David's sum is 3.

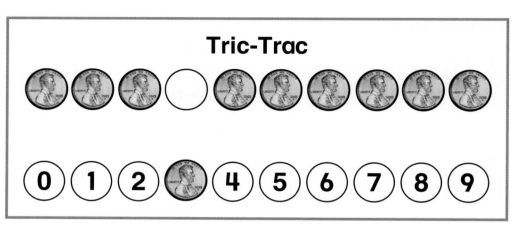

This is one way David can cover his sum.

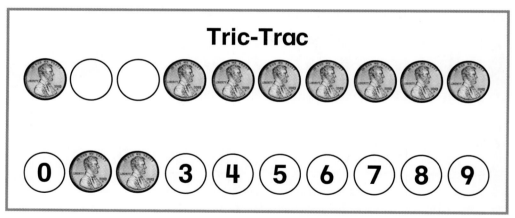

This is another way David can cover his sum.

Calculators

Calculators

A **calculator** is a tool that can help you do many things. You can use it to count, add, subtract, multiply, and divide. Not all calculators are alike.

● Here is one type of calculator.

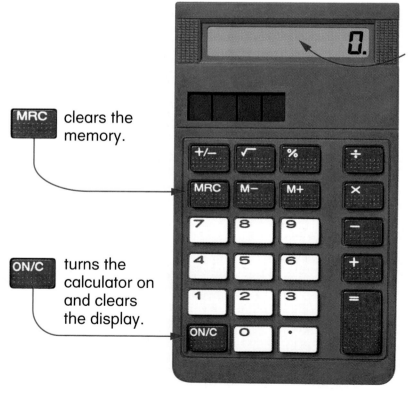

This is called the display window.

MRC clears the memory.

ON/C turns the calculator on and clears the display.

Here is another type of calculator.

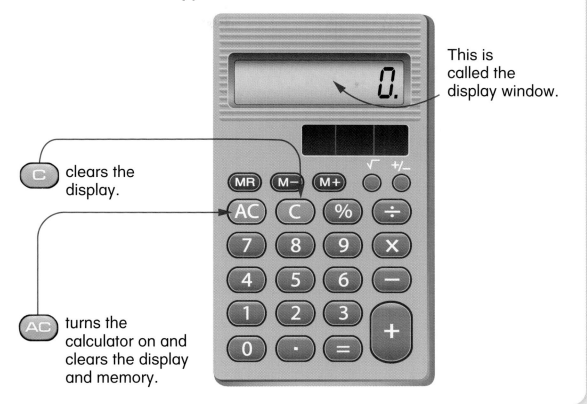

This is called the display window.

C clears the display.

AC turns the calculator on and clears the display and memory.

You can **skip count** up or back on a calculator.

- Use [calculator] to skip count. Start at 1. Count up by 2s.

Program the calculator	Keys to Press	Display
Clear the display.	ON/C	0.
Enter the starting number.	1	1.
Tell it to count up by a number.	+ 2	2.
Tell it to skip to the next number.	=	3.
Tell it to skip to the next number.	=	5.
Tell it to skip to the next number.	=	7.

You can count back by pressing ☐ instead of +.

Note

When skip counting beginning with a negative number, it is necessary to enter the start number and then press the [+/−] key to make the number negative.

Use 🖩 to skip count. Start at 1. Count up by 2s.

Program the calculator	Keys to Press	Display
Clear the display.	(AC)	0.
Tell it to count up by a number.	2 (+) (+)	κ 2.+
Enter the starting number.	1	κ 1.+
Tell it to skip to the next number.	(=)	κ 3.+
Tell it to skip to the next number.	(=)	κ 5.+
Tell it to skip to the next number.	(=)	κ 7.+

You can count back by pressing ⊖⊖ instead of (+)(+).

Note

Always clear the calculator display before you start something new.

The keys for the **basic operations** are on every calculator.

● These tables show addition and subtraction problems.

Operation	Problem	Key Sequence	Display
Addition	2 + 4	2 [+] 4 [=]	6.
Addition	23 + 19	23 [+] 19 [=]	42.

Operation	Problem	Key Sequence	Display
Subtraction	10 − 7	10 [−] 7 [=]	3.
Subtraction	51 − 16	51 [−] 16 [=]	35.

Note

Ask yourself if the number in the display makes sense. This helps you know if you pressed a wrong key or made another mistake.

These tables show multiplication and division problems.

Operation	Problem	Key Sequence	Display
Multiplication	2 × 5	2 ⊗ 5 ⊜	10.
Multiplication	6 × 14	6 ⊗ 14 ⊜	84.

Operation	Problem	Key Sequence	Display
Division	10 ÷ 2	10 ⊘ 2 ⊜	5.
Division	92 ÷ 4	92 ⊘ 4 ⊜	23.

Try It Together

Play *Beat the Calculator* on pages 124–125.

California Content Standards

The California Mathematics Content Standards describe what every child in California can and needs to learn in mathematics. These standards are listed here for your reference.

Grade 1 Standards

Pages CA3–CA6

Measurement and Geometry 2.3 Give and follow directions about location.

Measurement and Geometry 2.4 Arrange and describe objects in space by proximity, position, and direction (e.g., near, far, below, above, up, down, behind, in front of, next to, left or right of).

Pages CA7-CA10

Measurement and Geometry 2.1 Identify, describe, and compare triangles, rectangles, squares, and circles, including the faces of three-dimensional objects.

Page CA11

Number Sense 2.7 Find the sum of three one-digit numbers.

Algebra and Functions 1.3 Create problem situations that might lead to given number sentences involving addition and subtraction.

Measurement and Geometry 1.1 Compare the length, weight, and volume of two or more objects by using direct comparison or a nonstandard unit.

Pages CA12–CA17

Number Sense 2.7 Find the sum of three one-digit numbers.

Algebra and Functions 1.3 Create problem situations that might lead to given number sentences involving addition and subtraction.

Page CA18–CA19

Number Sense 1.0 Students understand and use numbers up to 100.

Algebra and Functions 1.3 Create problem situations that might lead to given number sentences involving addition and subtraction.

Pages CA20–CA21

Measurement and Geometry 1.2 Tell time to the nearest half hour and relate time to events (e.g., before/after, shorter/longer).

Pages 2–5

Number Sense 1.0 Students understand and use numbers up to 100.

Number Sense 1.1 Count, read, and write whole numbers to 100.

Grade 2 Standards

Pages CA7–CA10

Measurement and Geometry 2.2 Put shapes together and take them apart to form other shapes (e.g., two congruent right triangles can be arranged to form a rectangle).

Page CA11

Statistics, Data Analysis, and Probability 1.4 Ask and answer simple questions related to data representations.

Page CA18–23

Measurement and Geometry 1.5 Determine the duration of intervals of time in hours (e.g., 11:00 a.m. to 4:00 p.m.).

Pages CA18–CA21

Statistics, Data Analysis, and Probability 1.2 Represent the same data set in more than one way (e.g., bar graphs and charts with tallies).

Pages 2–5

Number Sense 1.1 Count, read, and write whole numbers to 1,000 and identify the place value for each digit.

165A

Grade 1 Standards

Pages 6, 7

Number Sense 1.0 Students understand and use numbers up to 100.

Number Sense 1.1 Count, read, and write whole numbers to 100.

Number Sense 2.4 Count by 2s, 5s, and 10s to 100.

Page 8

Number Sense 1.1 Count, read, and write whole numbers up to 100.

Number Sense 2.3 Identify one more than, one less than, 10 more than, and 10 less than a given number.

Number Sense 2.4 Count by 2s, 5s, and 10s to 100.

Page 9

Number Sense 1.2 Compare and order whole numbers to 100 by using the symbols for less than, equal to, or greater than ($<$, $=$, $>$).

Pages 10, 11

Number Sense 1.0 Students understand and use numbers up to 100.

Number Sense 1.1 Count, read, and write whole numbers to 100.

Number Sense 1.4 Count and group objects in ones and tens (e.g., three groups of 10 and 4 equals 34, or 30 + 4).

Pages 12–15

Mathematical Reasoning 1.2 Use tools, such as manipulatives or sketches, to model problems.

Grade 2 Standards

Pages 6–8

Number Sense 1.1 Count, read, and write whole numbers to 1,000 and identify the place value for each digit.

Page 9

Number Sense 1.3 Order and compare whole numbers to 1,000 by using the symbols $<$, $=$, $>$.

Pages 10, 11

Number Sense 1.0 Students understand the relationship between numbers, quantities, and place value in whole numbers up to 1,000.

Number Sense 1.1 Count, read, and write whole numbers to 1,000 and identify the place value for each digit.

Number Sense 1.2 Use words, models, and expanded forms (e.g., 45 = 4 tens + 5) to represent numbers (to 1,000).

Pages 12–15

Number Sense 4.0 Students understand that fractions and decimals may refer to parts of a set and parts of a whole.

Number Sense 4.1 Recognize, name, and compare unit fractions from $\frac{1}{12}$ to $\frac{1}{12}$.

Number Sense 4.2 Recognize fractions of a whole and parts of a group (e.g., one-fourth of a pie, two-thirds of 15 balls).

Mathematical Reasoning 1.2 Use tools, such as manipulatives or sketches, to model problems.

Pages 14, 15

Number Sense 4.3 Know that when all fractional parts are included, such as four-fourths, the result is equal to the whole and to one.

165B

California Content Standards

 CALIFORNIA

Grade 1 Standards

Page 16

Number Sense 1.3 Represent equivalent forms of the same number through the use of physical models, diagrams, and number expressions (to 20) (e.g., 8 may be represented as 4 + 4, 5 + 3, 2 + 2 + 2 + 2, 10 − 2, 11 − 3).

Mathematical Reasoning 1.2 Use tools, such as manipulatives or sketches, to model problems.

Pages 17–19

Number Sense 1.0 Students understand and use numbers up to 100.

Number Sense 1.1 Count, read, and write whole numbers to 100.

Pages 20, 21

Number Sense 1.0 Students understand and use numbers up to 100.

Algebra and Functions 1.0 Students use number sentences with operational symbols and expressions to solve problems.

Pages 22–24

Number Sense 2.0 Students demonstrate the meaning of addition and subtraction and use these operations to solve problems.

Algebra and Functions 1.0 Students use number sentences with operational symbols and expressions to solve problems.

Number Sense 2.5 Show the meaning of addition (putting together, increasing) and subtraction (taking away, comparing, finding the difference).

Algebra and Functions 1.2 Understand the meaning of the symbols +, −, =.

Mathematical Reasoning 1.2 Use tools, such as manipulatives or sketches, to model problems.

Pages 25–27

Number Sense 2.1 Know the addition facts (sums to 20) and the corresponding subtraction facts and commit them to memory.

Algebra and Functions 1.2 Understand the meaning of the symbols +, −, =.

Mathematical Reasoning 1.2 Use tools, such as manipulatives or sketches, to model problems.

Number Sense 2.2 Use the inverse relationship between addition and subtraction to solve problems.

Grade 2 Standards

Page 16

Number Sense 1.2 Use words, models, and expanded forms (e.g., 45 = 4 tens + 5) to represent numbers (to 1,000).

Mathematical Reasoning 1.2 Use tools, such as manipulatives or sketches, to model problems.

Pages 17–20

Number Sense 1.1 Count, read, and write whole numbers to 1,000 and identify the place value for each digit.

Pages 22–24

Number Sense 2.0 Students estimate, calculate, and solve problems involving addition and subtraction of two- and three-digit numbers.

Number Sense 2.2 Find the sum or difference of two whole numbers up to three digits long.

Mathematical Reasoning 1.2 Use tools, such as manipulatives or sketches, to model problems.

Pages 25–27

Number Sense 2.0 Students estimate, calculate, and solve problems involving addition and subtraction of two- and three-digit numbers.

Number Sense 2.2 Find the sum or difference of two whole numbers up to three digits long.

Number Sense 2.1 Understand and use the inverse relationship between addition and subtraction (e.g., an opposite number sentence for 8 + 6 = 14 is 14 − 6 = 8) to solve problems and check solutions.

Algebra and Functions 1.1 Use the commutative and associative rules to simplify mental calculations and to check results.

Mathematical Reasoning 1.2 Use tools, such as manipulatives or sketches, to model problems.

 165C

Grade 1 Standards

Page 28
Number Sense 2.5 Show the meaning of addition (putting together, increasing) and subtraction (taking away, comparing, finding the difference).

Number Sense 2.6 Solve addition and subtraction problems with one- and two-digit numbers (e.g., 5 + 58 = __).

Number Sense 1.4 Count and group objects in ones and tens (e.g., three groups of 10 and 4 equals 34, or 30 + 4).

Algebra and Functions 1.2 Understand the meaning of the symbols +, −, =.

Mathematical Reasoning 1.2 Use tools, such as manipulatives or sketches, to model problems.

Page 29
Number Sense 2.6 Solve addition and subtraction problems with one- and two-digit numbers (e.g., 5 + 58 = __).

Algebra and Functions 1.2 Understand the meaning of the symbols +, −, =.

Mathematical Reasoning 1.2 Use tools, such as manipulatives or sketches, to model problems.

Page 30
Number Sense 1.4 Count and group objects in ones and tens (e.g., three groups of 10 and 4 equals 34, or 30 + 4).

Number Sense 2.6 Solve addition and subtraction problems with one- and two-digit numbers (e.g., 5 + 58 = __).

Algebra and Functions 1.2 Understand the meaning of the symbols +, −, =.

Pages 30A–30B
Number Sense 2.6 Solve addition and subtraction problems with one-and two-digit numbers (e.g., 5 + 58 = __).

Grade 2 Standards

Page 27
Mathematical Reasoning 3.0 Students note connections between one problem and another.

Page 28
Number Sense 2.0 Students estimate, calculate, and solve problems involving addition and subtraction of two- and three-digit numbers.

Number Sense 2.2 Find the sum or difference of two whole numbers up to three digits long.

Mathematical Reasoning 1.2 Use tools, such as manipulatives or sketches, to model problems.

Page 29
Number Sense 2.0 Students estimate, calculate, and solve problems involving addition and subtraction of two- and three-digit numbers.

Number Sense 2.2 Find the sum or difference of two whole numbers up to three digits long.

Mathematical Reasoning 1.2 Use tools, such as manipulatives or sketches, to model problems.

Page 30
Number Sense 2.0 Students estimate, calculate, and solve problems involving addition and subtraction of two- and three-digit numbers.

Number Sense 2.2 Find the sum or difference of two whole numbers up to three digits long.

Page 30A–30B
Number Sense 2.0 Students estimate, calculate, and solve problems involving addition and subtraction of two- and three-digit numbers.

Number Sense 2.2 Find the sum or difference of two whole numbers up to three digits long.

California Content Standards

Page 31

Number Sense 1.4 Count and group objects in ones and tens (e.g., three groups of 10 and 4 equals 34, or 30 + 4).

Number Sense 2.5 Show the meaning of addition (putting together, increasing) and subtraction (taking away, comparing, finding the difference).

Number Sense 2.6 Solve addition and subtraction problems with one- and two-digit numbers (e.g., 5 + 58 = __).

Algebra and Functions 1.2 Understand the meaning of the symbols +, −, =.

Mathematical Reasoning 1.2 Use tools, such as manipulatives or sketches, to model problems.

Pages 32, 33

Number Sense 2.6 Solve addition and subtraction problems with one- and two-digit numbers (e.g., 5 + 58 = __).

Algebra and Functions 1.2 Understand the meaning of the symbols +, −, =.

Mathematical Reasoning 1.2 Use tools, such as manipulatives or sketches, to model problems.

Pages 34, 35

Number Sense 2.6 Solve addition and subtraction problems with one- and two-digit numbers (e.g., 5 + 58 = __).

Algebra and Functions 1.2 Understand the meaning of the symbols +, −, =.

Pages 35A–35B

Number Sense 2.6 Solve addition and subtraction problems with one-and two-digit numbers (e.g., 5 + 58 = __).

Page 36

Mathematical Reasoning 1.2 Use tools, such as manipulatives or sketches, to model problems.

Page 31

Number Sense 2.0 Students estimate, calculate, and solve problems involving addition and subtraction of two- and three-digit numbers.

Number Sense 2.2 Find the sum or difference of two whole numbers up to three digits long.

Mathematical Reasoning 1.2 Use tools, such as manipulatives or sketches, to model problems.

Pages 32, 33

Number Sense 2.0 Students estimate, calculate, and solve problems involving addition and subtraction of two- and three-digit numbers.

Number Sense 2.2 Find the sum or difference of two whole numbers up to three digits long.

Mathematical Reasoning 1.2 Use tools, such as manipulatives or sketches, to model problems.

Pages 34, 35

Number Sense 2.0 Students estimate, calculate, and solve problems involving addition and subtraction of two- and three-digit numbers.

Number Sense 2.2 Find the sum or difference of two whole numbers up to three digits long.

Pages 35A–35B

Number Sense 2.2 Find the sum or difference of two whole numbers up to three digits long.

Page 36

Number Sense 3.0 Students model and solve simple problems involving multiplication and division.

Number Sense 3.1 Use repeated addition, arrays, and counting by multiples to do multiplication.

Number Sense 3.2 Use repeated subtraction, equal sharing, and forming equal groups with remainders to do division.

Mathematical Reasoning 1.2 Use tools, such as manipulatives or sketches, to model problems.

Grade 1 Standards

Pages 37, 38

Mathematical Reasoning 1.2 Use tools, such as manipulatives or sketches, to model problems.

Pages 40–44

Statistics, Data Analysis, and Probability 1.0 Students organize, represent, and compare data by category on simple graphs and charts.

Statistics, Data Analysis, and Probability 1.2 Represent and compare data (e.g., largest, smallest, most often, least often) by using pictures, bar graphs, tally charts, and picture graphs.

Pages 45, 46

Statistics, Data Analysis, and Probability 1.0 Students organize, represent, and compare data by category on simple graphs and charts.

Statistics, Data Analysis, and Probability 1.2 Represent and compare data (e.g., largest, smallest, most often, least often) by using pictures, bar graphs, tally charts, and picture graphs.

Pages 47, 48

Mathematical Reasoning 1.2 Use tools, such as manipulatives or sketches, to model problems.

Grade 2 Standards

Pages 37, 38

Number Sense 3.0 Students model and solve simple problems involving multiplication and division.

Number Sense 3.1 Use repeated addition, arrays, and counting by multiples to do multiplication.

Number Sense 3.2 Use repeated subtraction, equal sharing, and forming equal groups with remainders to do division.

Number Sense 3.3 Know the multiplication tables of 2s, 5s, and 10s (to "times 10") and commit them to memory.

Algebra and Functions 1.1 Use the commutative and associative rules to simplify mental calculations and to check results.

Mathematical Reasoning 1.2 Use tools, such as manipulatives or sketches, to model problems.

Pages 40, 41

Statistics, Data Analysis, and Probability 1.3 Identify features of data sets (range and mode).

Pages 40–44

Statistics, Data Analysis, and Probability 1.0 Students collect numerical data and record, organize, display, and interpret the data on bar graphs and other representations.

Statistics, Data Analysis, and Probability 1.1 Record numerical data in systematic ways, keeping track of what has been counted.

Statistics, Data Analysis, and Probability 1.2 Represent the same data set in more than one way (e.g., bar graphs and charts with tallies).

Statistics, Data Analysis, and Probability 1.4 Ask and answer simple questions related to data representations.

Pages 45, 46

Statistics, Data Analysis, and Probability 1.0 Students collect numerical data and record, organize, display, and interpret the data on bar graphs and other representations.

Statistics, Data Analysis, and Probability 1.1 Record numerical data in systematic ways, keeping track of what has been counted.

Statistics, Data Analysis, and Probability 1.3 Identify features of data sets (range and mode).

Statistics, Data Analysis, and Probability 1.4 Ask and answer simple questions related to data representations.

Algebra and Functions 1.3 Solve addition and subtraction problems by using data from simple charts, picture graphs, and number sentences.

Pages 47, 48

Mathematical Reasoning 1.2 Use tools, such as manipulatives or sketches, to model problems.

California Content Standards

Grade 1 Standards

Pages 50, 51

Measurement and Geometry 2.0 Students identify common geometric figures, classify them by common attributes, and describe their relative position or their location in space.

Pages 52–55

Measurement and Geometry 2.1 Identify, describe, and compare triangles, rectangles, squares, and circles, including the faces of three-dimensional objects.

Measurement and Geometry 2.2 Classify familiar plane and solid objects by common attributes, such as color, position, shape, size, roundness, or number of corners, and explain which attributes are being used for classification.

Pages 56, 57

Measurement and Geometry 2.1 Identify, describe, and compare triangles, rectangles, squares, and circles, including the faces of three-dimensional objects.

Measurement and Geometry 2.2 Classify familiar plane and solid objects by common attributes, such as color, position, shape, size, roundness, or number of corners, and explain which attributes are being used for classification.

Pages 58–59

Measurement and Geometry 2.0 Students identify common geometric figures, classify them by common attributes, and describe their relative position or their location in space.

Measurement and Geometry 2.1 Identify, describe, and compare triangles, rectangles, squares, and circles, including the faces of three-dimensional objects.

Page 60

Measurement and Geometry 2.0 Students identify common geometric figures, classify them by common attributes, and describe their relative position or their location in space.

Pages 62–67

Measurement and Geometry 1.0 Students use direct comparison and nonstandard units to describe the measurement of objects.

Grade 2 Standards

Pages 50, 51

Measurement and Geometry 2.0 Students identify and describe the attributes of common figures in the plane and of common objects in space.

Pages 52–55

Measurement and Geometry 2.0 Students identify and describe the attributes of common figures in the plane and of common objects in space.

Measurement and Geometry 2.1 Describe and classify plane and solid geometric shapes (e.g., circle, triangle, square, rectangle, sphere, pyramid, cube, rectangular prism) according to the number and shape of faces, edges, and vertices.

Pages 56–59

Measurement and Geometry 2.0 Students identify and describe the attributes of common figures in the plane and of common objects in space.

Measurement and Geometry 2.1 Describe and classify plane and solid geometric shapes (e.g., circle, triangle, square, rectangle, sphere, pyramid, cube, rectangular prism) according to the number and shape of faces, edges, and vertices.

Page 60

Measurement and Geometry 2.0 Students identify and describe the attributes of common figures in the plane and of common objects in space.

Pages 62–67

Measurement and Geometry 1.0 Students understand that measurement is accomplished by identifying a unit of measure, iterating (repeating) that unit, and comparing it to the item to be measured.

Measurement and Geometry 1.1 Measure the length of objects by iterating (repeating) a nonstandard or standard unit.

Pages 65, 66

Measurement and Geometry 1.3 Measure the length of an object to the nearest inch and/or centimeter.

Grade 1 Standards

Pages 70–72

Measurement and Geometry 1.0 Students use direct comparison and nonstandard units to describe the measurement of objects.

Pages 78–83

Measurement and Geometry 1.2 Tell time to the nearest half hour and relate time to events (e.g., before/after, shorter/longer).

Pages 88–90

Number Sense 1.5 Identify and know the value of coins and show different combinations of coins that equal the same value.

Grade 2 Standards

Pages 68, 69

Measurement and Geometry 1.3 Measure the length of an object to the nearest inch and/or centimeter.

Measurement and Geometry 1.0 Students understand that measurement is accomplished by identifying a unit of measure, iterating (repeating) that unit, and comparing it to the item to be measured.

Pages 70–72

Measurement and Geometry 1.0 Students understand that measurement is accomplished by identifying a unit of measure, iterating (repeating) that unit, and comparing it to the item to be measured.

Pages 73–76

Measurement and Geometry 1.0 Students understand that measurement is accomplished by identifying a unit of measure, iterating (repeating) that unit, and comparing it to the item to be measured.

Pages 78–83

Measurement and Geometry 1.4 Tell time to the nearest quarter hour and know relationships of time (e.g., minutes in an hour, days in a month, weeks in a year).

Pages 84–86

Measurement and Geometry 1.4 Tell time to the nearest quarter hour and know relationships of time (e.g., minutes in an hour, days in a month, weeks in a year).

Page 87

Measurement and Geometry 1.0 Students understand that measurement is accomplished by identifying a unit of measure, iterating (repeating) that unit, and comparing it to the item to be measured.

Pages 88–90

Number Sense 5.0 Students model and solve problems by representing, adding, and subtracting amounts of money.

Number Sense 5.1 Solve problems using combinations of coins and bills.

Number Sense 5.2 Know and use the decimal notation and the dollar and cent symbols for money.

Page 90

Number Sense 4.0 Students understand that fractions and decimals may refer to parts of a set and parts of a whole.

California Content Standards

Grade1 Standards

Pages 92–94

Number Sense 3.0 Students use estimation strategies in computation and problem solving that involve numbers that use the ones, tens, and hundreds places.

Number Sense 3.1 Make reasonable estimates when comparing larger or smaller numbers.

Pages 96, 97

Statistics, Data Analysis, and Probability 2.1 Describe, extend, and explain ways to get to a next element in simple repeating patterns (e.g., rhythmic, numeric, color, and shape).

Statistics, Data Analysis, and Probability 2.0 Students sort objects and create and describe patterns by numbers, shapes, sizes, rhythms, or colors.

Pages 98, 99

Number Sense 2.4 Count by 2s, 5s, and 10s to 100.

Number Sense 2.6 Solve addition and subtraction problems with one- and two-digit numbers (e.g., 5 + 58 = __).

Statistics, Data Analysis, and Probability 2.1 Describe, extend, and explain ways to get to a next element in simple repeating patterns (e.g., rhythmic, numeric, color, and shape).

Number Sense 2.0 Students demonstrate the meaning of addition and subtraction and use these operations to solve problems.

Statistics, Data Analysis, and Probability 2.0 Students sort objects and create and describe patterns by numbers, shapes, sizes, rhythms, or colors.

Pages 100–102

Number Sense 2.0 Students demonstrate the meaning of addition and subtraction and use these operations to solve problems.

Pages 103–106

Statistics, Data Analysis, and Probability 2.0 Students sort objects and create and describe patterns by numbers, shapes, sizes, rhythms, or colors.

Statistics, Data Analysis, and Probability 2.1 Describe, extend, and explain ways to get to a next element in simple repeating patterns (e.g., rhythmic, numeric, color, and shape).

Grade 2 Standards

Pages 92–94

Number Sense 2.0 Students estimate, calculate, and solve problems involving addition and subtraction of two- and three-digit numbers.

Number Sense 2.2 Find the sum or difference of two whole numbers up to three digits long.

Number Sense 6.0 Students use estimation strategies in computation and problem solving that involve numbers that use the ones, tens, hundreds, and thousands places.

Pages 96, 97

Statistics, Data Analysis, and Probability 2.0 Students demonstrate an understanding of patterns and how patterns grow and describe them in general ways.

Statistics, Data Analysis, and Probability 2.1 Recognize, describe, and extend patterns and determine a next term in linear patterns (e.g., 4, 8, 12 . . . ; the number of ears on one horse, two horses, three horses, four horses).

Statistics, Data Analysis, and Probability 2.2 Solve problems involving simple number patterns.

Pages 98, 99

Number Sense 2.2 Find the sum or difference of two whole numbers up to three digits long.

Statistics, Data Analysis, and Probability 2.0 Students demonstrate an understanding of patterns and how patterns grow and describe them in general ways.

Statistics, Data Analysis, and Probability 2.1 Recognize, describe, and extend patterns and determine a next term in linear patterns (e.g., 4, 8, 12 . . . ; the number of ears on one horse, two horses, three horses, four horses).

Statistics, Data Analysis, and Probability 2.2 Solve problems involving simple number patterns.

Pages 100–102

Number Sense 2.2 Find the sum or difference of two whole numbers up to three digits long.

Pages 103–106

Statistics, Data Analysis, and Probability 2.0 Students demonstrate an understanding of patterns and how patterns grow and describe them in general ways.

Grade 1 Standards

Pages 108–111

Number Sense 2.0 Students demonstrate the meaning of addition and subtraction and use these operations to solve problems.

Number Sense 2.5 Show the meaning of addition (putting together, increasing) and subtraction (taking away, comparing, finding the difference).

Number Sense 2.6 Solve addition and subtraction problems with one- and two-digit numbers (e.g., $5 + 58 = \_\_$).

Algebra and Functions 1.0 Students use number sentences with operational symbols and expressions to solve problems.

Algebra and Functions 1.1 Write and solve number sentences from problem situations that express relationships involving addition and subtraction.

Mathematical Reasoning 1.2 Use tools, such as manipulatives or sketches, to model problems.

Pages 112, 113

Algebra and Functions 1.0 Students use number sentences with operational symbols and expressions to solve problems.

Mathematical Reasoning 1.2 Use tools, such as manipulatives or sketches, to model problems.

Pages 114, 115

Algebra and Functions 1.0 Students use number sentences with operational symbols and expressions to solve problems.

Mathematical Reasoning 1.2 Use tools, such as manipulatives or sketches, to model problems.

Grade 2 Standards

Pages 108–111

Number Sense 2.0 Students estimate, calculate, and solve problems involving addition and subtraction of two- and three-digit numbers.

Number Sense 2.1 Understand and use the inverse relationship between addition and subtraction (e.g., an opposite number sentence for $8 + 6 = 14$ is $14 - 6 = 8$) to solve problems and check solutions.

Algebra and Functions 1.0 Students model, represent, and interpret number relationships to create and solve problems involving addition and subtraction.

Algebra and Functions 1.2 Relate problem situations to number sentences involving addition and subtraction.

Mathematical Reasoning 1.2 Use tools, such as manipulatives or sketches, to model problems.

Pages 112, 113

Mathematical Reasoning 1.2 Use tools, such as manipulatives or sketches, to model problems.

Number Sense 3.0 Students model and solve simple problems involving multiplication and division.

Number Sense 3.1 Use repeated addition, arrays, and counting by multiples to do multiplication.

Pages 114, 115

Number Sense 3.0 Students model and solve simple problems involving multiplication and division.

Number Sense 3.2 Use repeated subtraction, equal sharing, and forming equal groups with remainders to do division.

Mathematical Reasoning 1.2 Use tools, such as manipulatives or sketches, to model problems.

Page 115

Measurement and Geometry 2.1 Describe and classify plane and solid geometric shapes (e.g., circle, triangle, square, rectangle, sphere, pyramid, cube, rectangular prism) according to the number and shape of faces, edges, and vertices.

California Content Standards

Grade 1 Standards

Pages 116–118

Number Sense 2.0 Students demonstrate the meaning of addition and subtraction and use these operations to solve problems.

Number Sense 2.5 Show the meaning of addition (putting together, increasing) and subtraction (taking away, comparing, finding the difference).

Number Sense 2.6 Solve addition and subtraction problems with one- and two-digit numbers (e.g., $5 + 58 =$ __).

Algebra and Functions 1.0 Students use number sentences with operational symbols and expressions to solve problems.

Algebra and Functions 1.1 Write and solve number sentences from problem situations that express relationships involving addition and subtraction.

Mathematical Reasoning 1.2 Use tools, such as manipulatives or sketches, to model problems.

Pages 120, 121

Number Sense 2.6 Solve addition and subtraction problems with one- and two-digit numbers (e.g., $5 + 58 =$ __).

Pages 122, 123

Number Sense 1.2 Compare and order whole numbers to 100 by using the symbols for less than, equal to, or greater than ($<$, $=$, $>$).

Number Sense 2.1 Know the addition facts (sums to 20) and the corresponding subtraction facts and commit them to memory.

Pages 124–125

Number Sense 2.1 Know the addition facts (sums to 20) and the corresponding subtraction facts and commit them to memory.

Pages 126, 127

Number Sense 1.2 Compare and order whole numbers to 100 by using the symbols for less than, equal to, or greater than ($<$, $=$, $>$).

Number Sense 2.3 Identify one more than, one less than, 10 more than, and 10 less than a given number.

Pages 128, 129

Number Sense 1.5 Identify and know the value of coins and show different combinations of coins that equal the same value.

Grade 2 Standards

Pages 116–118

Number Sense 2.0 Students estimate, calculate, and solve problems involving addition and subtraction of two- and three-digit numbers.

Number Sense 2.2 Find the sum or difference of two whole numbers up to three digits long.

Algebra and Functions 1.0 Students model, represent, and interpret number relationships to create and solve problems involving addition and subtraction.

Algebra and Functions 1.2 Relate problem situations to number sentences involving addition and subtraction.

Mathematical Reasoning 1.2 Use tools, such as manipulatives or sketches, to model problems.

Pages 120, 121

Number Sense 2.2 Find the sum or difference of two whole numbers up to three digits long.

Pages 122, 123

Number Sense 1.3 Order and compare whole numbers to 1,000 by using the symbols $<$, $=$, $>$.

Pages 122–125

Number Sense 2.2 Find the sum or difference of two whole numbers up to three digits long.

Pages 126, 127

Number Sense 1.0 Students understand the relationship between numbers, quantities, and place value in whole numbers up to 1,000.

Pages 128, 129

Number Sense 5.0 Students model and solve problems by representing, adding, and subtracting amounts of money.

Number Sense 5.1 Solve problems using combinations of coins and bills.

Grade 1 Standards

Pages 130, 131

Number Sense 2.1 Know the addition facts (sums to 20) and the corresponding subtraction facts and commit them to memory.

Number Sense 2.6 Solve addition and subtraction problems with one-and two-digit numbers (e.g., 5 + 58 = __).

Number Sense 2.5 Show the meaning of addition (putting together, increasing) and subtraction (taking away, comparing, finding the difference).

Pages 132, 133

Number Sense 1.0 Students understand and use numbers up to 100.

Number Sense 1.1 Count, read, and write whole numbers to 100.

Pages 134, 135

Number Sense 2.6 Solve addition and subtraction problems with one- and two-digit numbers (e.g., 5 + 58 = __).

Pages 136, 137

Number Sense 2.6 Solve addition and subtraction problems with one- and two-digit numbers (e.g., 5 + 58 = __).

Pages 138, 139

Number Sense 1.3 Represent equivalent forms of the same number through the use of physical models, diagrams, and number expressions (to 20) (e.g., 8 may be represented as 4 + 4, 5 + 3, 2 + 2 + 2 + 2, 10 − 2, 11 − 3).

Pages 140, 141

Number Sense 2.6 Solve addition and subtraction problems with one- and two-digit numbers (e.g., 5 + 58 = __).

Mathematical Reasoning 1.2 Use tools, such as manipulatives or sketches, to model problems.

Pages 142, 143

Number Sense 1.1 Count, read, and write whole numbers to 100.

Number Sense 2.6 Solve addition and subtraction problems with one-and two-digit numbers (e.g., 5 + 58 = __).

Grade 2 Standards

Pages 130, 131

Number Sense 2.2 Find the sum or difference of two whole numbers up to three digits long.

Pages 132, 133

Number Sense 1.0 Students understand the relationship between numbers, quantities, and place value in whole numbers up to 1,000.

Number Sense 1.2 Use words, models, and expanded forms (e.g., 45 = 4 tens + 5) to represent numbers (to 1,000).

Pages 134, 135

Number Sense 2.0 Students estimate, calculate, and solve problems involving addition and subtraction of two- and three-digit numbers.

Number Sense 2.2 Find the sum or difference of two whole numbers up to three digits long.

Number Sense 2.3 Use mental arithmetic to find the sum or difference of two two-digit numbers.

Pages 136, 137

Number Sense 2.2 Find the sum or difference of two whole numbers up to three digits long.

Pages 138, 139

Number Sense 1.2 Use words, models, and expanded forms (e.g., 45 = 4 tens + 5) to represent numbers (to 1,000).

Pages 140, 141

Number Sense 2.2 Find the sum or difference of two whole numbers up to three digits long.

Mathematical Reasoning 1.2 Use tools, such as manipulatives or sketches, to model problems.

Pages 142, 143

Number Sense 1.0 Students understand the relationship between numbers, quantities, and place value in whole numbers up to 1,000.

California Content Standards

Index

Index

Index